# GARDEN OF GRACE

# Garden of Grace

## A season of healing from a broken place

BY AMELIA RAYMOND

*Illustrations By Esther Job*

Ingram Sparks

*I dedicate this to my mother and grandmother. For my mother, thank you for giving me my middle name of Rose, and my love for the garden. To my grandmother, thank you for always believing in me and encouraging me to write.*

-With love, Amelia Rose

Copyright © 2022 by Amelia Raymond

All rights reserved. No part of this book may be reproduced in any manner whatsoever without written permission except in the case of brief quotations embodied in critical articles and reviews.

First Printing, 2022

Scripture quotations marked (NLT) are taken from the Holy Bible, New Living Translation, copyright © 1996, 2004, 2007 by Tyndale House Foundation. Used by permission of Tyndale House Publishers, Inc., Carol Stream, IL 60188. All rights reserved.

INTRODUCTION

When I was a little girl I used to read Beatrix Potter books. They became a large part of my childhood and many memories were spent dreaming of the characters in the book. Every year my family would take a trip away from our small English village and go to the Isle of White. There we stayed in a beautiful little cottage and the garden was the place I spent most of my time. I imagined I was in the Beatrix Potter books playing with 'Peter Rabbit' (Potter, 1901) and creating stories of my own. One night, we watched the Beatrix Potter movie about how she became an author. My eyes widened, my heart sang, at the age of seven, I knew that one day, I would write many books. Soon I began writing stories that involved rabbits, fairies, and princesses. As time went on my stories became more elaborate. I have written many novels, but this is the first story I wish to share. Rather than sharing stories of my imagination, I hope to share the story that has been on my heart ever since I was a little girl. This story is about the garden of *your* heart. Turning *your* eyes towards Jesus and understanding the incredible Grace God has for your life. I will unpack the analogy of the *garden* and bring insight to you about how my life was transformed by the Father's Grace. Stories of truth, and stories of Grace, God has awakened my heart to new promises and I want to share this beautiful love with you. *'Garden of Grace'* will empower you to find your worth in Christ.

Beloved, you are worthy, you are beautiful and you are a treasured flower in the garden. You are unique, one of a kind, you have a purpose and you are here for a reason. Nothing can separate you from the Grace of God.

This book was written during a tough and painful season. While heartache lived within me, a beautiful touch of God came. This brought hope, restoration, and healing. This new season I stepped into was a season of Grace. It was at my darkest point that I discovered the wonderful, powerful and intense love that Christ has for His people. He is always with us, never leaving us or forsaking us. He loves us deeply and I hope this book will bring you an insight into this incredible love and joy. This book will challenge you, awaken new thoughts and encourage you to go deeper with your relationship with Christ.

You are God's beloved, He is reaching out to you, turn your eyes back to the *Garden of Grace*.

"For as the soil makes the sprout come up and a garden causes seeds to grow, so the Sovereign LORD will make righteousness and praise spring up before all nations."

(*NLT,* 1996, Isiah 61:11)

## CHAPTER ONE

THE HONEY BEE

**Part 1**

The garden was the most magical place on earth when I was a little girl. My childhood home was found in a small village in England. Our garden was never-ending, like a forest. It was vast, like the ocean. It was picturesque and a sight for sore eyes. There was a zip line that went from the top of the garden all the way through to the bottom. Trees covered the surroundings, with their tall, strong stance. I would always sit under them to seek shade from the sun on a warm British day. Daisies covered every inch of the grass. Making daisy chains became a favorite activity of mine. The most important part of the garden was at the very back. Deep, down within, was a hidden treasure. Past the tall trees and freshly trimmed bushes was our very own *Secret Garden.*

My mother used to read the story to me and I forever

held this novel and movie close to my heart. When I was around five years old, I decided that this hidden part of our garden was the real *Secret Garden.* My dear sister, Jayne, who was eight years old at the time, decided that it was the *fairy's secret garden* and there was only one way you would be accepted into this garden. I wanted more than anything to be accepted into this secret garden full of fairies and magic. So I asked her with great enthusiasm to tell me how I could get accepted into the fairy secret garden. As any eight-year-old sister would do, she played a harmless trick on me that has stuck with me for many years now. Looking back, I laughed and smiled at how sweet and innocent our games were.

As my sister gently grabbed my hand and guided me inside, through the kitchen we ran, sliding our socks across the tiles and into the front room. Our front room had big windows that let the sun intensely shine inside. I remember looking out at the brightness through the big windows and hoping the fairies would let me in on this incredible secret garden. Jayne held a jar of sweets out and told me that she was going to see if I could get into the garden. Placing some sweets into my right hand, she told me to hold the sweets tightly and ask the fairies if I was worthy of being a part of the secret garden. I closed my eyes and held them tightly in my hand. Softly I whispered into the warm British afternoon air if I could be accepted into the garden. Opening my eyes my sister told me to eat the sweets and to hold my hand out with the palm of my hand flat and facing the sky.

"Look closely at the lines on your palm, if this line is

long enough then you will be good enough for the fairy garden," Jayne said enthusiastically.

Hoping the lines on my palms were long enough I took a deep breath and asked her if they were. She took my hand and started to analyze it for a moment with a,

"Hmm, I see. Hmm, okay". Jayne said with a grim look on her face. Her eyes looked up at me and she told me the lines on my hand were not long enough, I was not accepted into the secret garden. She, however, allowed me to finish off the sweets jar. At the time, the sweets were actually just as exciting and the loss of acceptance to the fairy garden no longer crossed my mind, as the sweet taste of sugar touched my lips.

While this story makes me laugh and reminds me of the innocent, imaginative mind I once had, it got me thinking. Have you ever been told you were not good enough? Not brave enough? Smart enough? Strong enough? Kind enough? Generous enough? Grateful enough? The notion of *not being enough* is something everyone will face at one point in their lives. Whether it be like a five-year-old rejected from the fairy garden, or as an adult being cut from a job, or the loss of a romantic relationship. Whatever way you experience *not being good enough,* I need you to know the truth. You are enough, in fact, you are more than a conqueror. You are royalty. You are a daughter of the king. Your worth is found in your Father. Do not let anyone tell you that you are not enough, for you truly are a precious rose in the garden of Grace. Stand up, own your worth, and do not accept that you are not enough. You are in fact, more than enough.

**Part 2**

That same afternoon, I was back in the garden making daisy chains. I had a crown of flowers on my head and the honey bees were beginning to follow me. Our dear friend Amy was on her way to come and play in the garden with us. I began making a flower crown for her as well. As I held the flower crown in my hand and looked up to the sound of my friend arriving in the garden, I waved a big,

"Hello!"

Right as I waved my hand, the fluffy honey bee that had been following my flower crown stung me right on the palm of my hand. Quickly I ran to my mother and showed her the sting that had taken place. As she tended to my sting, it dawned on me that the honey bee had stung me right on the line that was *not enough* for the fairy garden. My young mind realized that when my hand swelled up from the sting, the lines actually looked long and I was now allowed into the garden. Instead of letting the sting bring me down, I used this as a way of turning my afternoon around. I decided I was *good enough* for the garden and off I went to play.

In life, when stings hit parts of our lives that are told they are not *good enough*, the sting can feel even worse. I encourage you to look at life from the perspective of a childlike faith. As a child turns a bee sting into something positive, so should you with the trials in your life. Whether it's a breakup, the loss of a job, or a friend letting you down, however you have been stung by the enemy, stand up and run back to the garden of grace, for you have always been worthy, always been welcomed, and will always be accepted.

Make the choice, turn your eyes to the Father, see your worth, you are good enough. Take the sting you felt today and turn it into something life-changing.

My friend, you are not just invited, but you are the guest of honor. The King's beloved, you are the dearest treasure in God's eyes. While earthly things will let you down, have a Godly mind and realize that you are invited and accepted by the King of Kings. Whatever you have done, wherever you have been, you are worthy. Walk in this freedom, walk in this Grace for the Lord is with you and waiting on you. Stand up, child, run back to where you belong, run back to the garden of Grace.

"The Lord protects those of childlike faith; I was facing death, and he saved me. Let my soul be at rest again, for the LORD has been good to me".

(*NLT*, 1996, Psalms 116:6).

## Reflection

1. What areas of your life do you have a childlike faith in?

2. How can you use your life experiences to bring guidance to others?

3. What aspect of your childhood brings you comfort? Think back to this time and see what God is revealing to you.

## CHAPTER TWO
THE APPLE TREE

## Part 1

By the time I was eight, I was living in a new house. This new home was in the same village but brought many new experiences within the garden. The day we went to look at the house before buying it, I saw the garden and I was mesmerized. While it was not as large as my previous garden, it was quite the sight for my young eyes. Upon further inspection, I noticed something beautiful. This hidden treasure within the garden was bright and orange. Something so simple, yet it caught my eye instantly. My heart gleamed with joy as I realized what it was. The bright orange object that shimmered in the afternoon sunshine was a cheerful, striking swing. The orange swing hung by a thin rope attached to an elegant apple tree. As the house tour continued, I stayed in the garden and looked at the swing as I dreamed of all the adventures I could go on with this one swing. There was something enchanting about swings to me. As a toddler, I would gravitate to the swings at the park. My mother would strap me into the swing and gently I would soar through the air. Something about gazing up into the clouds made my heart sing. The feeling of the wind softly brushing past my rosy cheeks brought a smile to the young innocent face.

Finally, I worked up the courage to hop on this lonely swing. Alone, in this foreign garden, while my family continued the tour of the house, I began dreaming of the new adventure I was about to embark on. The swing was tied to a sturdy branch that I put my complete trust in. Pushing my feet off the apple tree, I launched into the air and drifted gently down. Leaning my head back, I took a deep breath in and soaked up the afternoon sunshine. The clouds were extra fluffy that afternoon and my spirits were high. This was the house for me. No more house tours needed, this house was in fact, the one. I had a dreamlike experience on that swing which stayed with me for many days later. I constantly told my parents how much I adored that house, I promised them I would help around the garden if we got the house.

Moving day was an exciting time for me, setting up my new room and finally going back to the swing on the apple tree. As my small legs ran out around the side of the house and into the garden, there shining in the evening sun was my swing. I jumped on it with greater enthusiasm this time. Memories of my first encounter with this apple tree and swing came floating back and I never thought the rope could let me down. This apple tree was strong, the branches were sturdy. Nothing bad could happen. As I glided through the evening air, the smell of barbeque and blossoms filled my nose. As I leaned back to smile and soak in that blissful evening, my handsome apple tree swing let me down and the rope snapped. I quickly tumbled to the ground. Shock, confusion, and melancholy engulfed my mind. How could my apple tree swing let me down? With nothing but a sore bottom and a bruised leg, I ran inside to tell my father. He came up with a smart idea. He said it was not the tree that let me down, but the old rope. He ran into the garage and grabbed a long, dark, red rope that was the thickest rope I had ever seen. He headed for the garden with a ladder in his hand and the stronger, sturdier rope that was going to last me many years. As he attached the new rope to the tree, I laid on the grass and watched my father in admiration. He did not blame me for the rope breaking or get angry at me. Instead, he instantly had a solution for me. He already had the rope with him, I just needed to ask him for it. My father was an honorable man, always there to help, always there with a solution. The new rope was ready and the swing was now safe and secure, so I tried it again.

Going back to something that had once hurt me was not easy. I begin to lose trust, my faith faded away. Something I loved, dreamed about and cherished, let me down. Left me hurting and sad.

These moments in life can be sudden, you find what you once trusted or knew, snaps and you fall. Down you fall, sometimes down what seems like a never-ending spiral. As you look back and wonder how you could ever recover. How could you heal from such a tragedy? Have you ever found yourself on a lovely apple tree swing in life and abruptly that swing is taken from you? As a child, this was a harmless tree swing, what I didn't realize was that a life lesson was being taught to me at that moment, that would still impact me in my adulthood. This lesson came rushing back when I experienced a great loss as an adult, a sudden change in my life, a sudden change in what I knew. The rope broke, I was left hurt and lacked trust. I reached out to my Father who had the answer for me. All I needed to do was ask him for help. Whilst it was tempting to sit on the dirty floor after I had been hurt, let down, and forgotten, I needed to stand up and reach out to my Heavenly Father. Jesus already has the solution, He has something even better. You just need to ask. You do not need to sit in this place of despair any longer. Stand up, be strong, and go reach out to your Father. The solution He has in store for you is far greater than you could dream of. He has a rope that is stronger and sturdier that will not let you down.

"For I know the plans I have for you declares the Lord, plans to prosper you, not to harm you. To give you hope and a future"
(NLT, 1996 Jeremiah 29:11)

"In all things, God works for the good of those who love Him"
(NLT, 1996, Romans 8:28).

Beloved, your Father has incredible plans for your life.

Do not sit in fear, shame, or hurt. Reach out for you will be looked after. Sometimes we may be riding a swing with an old broken rope and not even know it. We may be unaware that there are bigger and better plans for our lives. Do not settle, stand up, reach out and ask your Father to guide your steps. To help you by showing you the way. If you ask Him, He will listen to you. His plans may not happen as we may have hoped, but they are good. He always works for the good of those who love him.

As my father placed his hand on my back, he said,

"Off you go, I am right here. Trust me, this rope won't let you down."

I hopped back onto the swing, smiling at my father, I launched myself into the air. Leaning back, my unbrushed brown hair scraped the ground and my heart flooded with joy. My apple tree swing was back. The breaking of the rope was not the breaking of me. I was strong, I was capable and I could get back onto the beautiful swing again.

### Part 2

Autumn was just a week away and my promise to help in the garden was now being fulfilled. I was given one job,

"Pick up all the fallen apples from the tree and throw them over the back fence."

My father would ask me.

Every Saturday afternoon after my morning ballet classes I would help in the garden, as promised. When I got home from ballet, I would put on my welly boots and warm jacket as I headed out of the garden with my father.

Our mission: clear out all the rotten apples. This was a big task, considering the number of apples that had fallen within a week. Half the garden was covered and the two of us got stuck into de-cluttering our beautiful garden. The task involved, picking up the apples, putting them into a bucket, and then heading to the far end of the garden to throw the apples over. This fence was not a small fence, it was three times the size of me. My weak young arms struggled to get every apple over. In fact, it was actually impossible for a small girl like me to throw 50 apples over a high fence. I needed my father to help me.

Have you ever noticed your heart is filled with things that feel like rotten apples? Have you ever been so angry and frustrated with someone that your garden within your heart has been filled with intense negativity? I have experienced moments where my heart feels heavy, my head is filled with rotten thoughts that lead me to take action in ways I would regret later on. Plotting ways to get back at a person who hurt you or finding ways to show them you are worth more can cause rotten apples to fall in your heart. Sometimes these rotten apples in our hearts lead us to act upon our emotions and behave out of character. Deep within my soul, rage fills up, rotten apples take over my garden and I am no longer myself, but a product of my emotions. Nothing I do can take such feelings away, the only way to get them out is to act upon these rotten feelings with more force than what they have on you. You need to pick them up and throw them out, hard. Harder than you've ever thrown. Swing your arms and launch those rotten feelings away from your fragile heart.

They do not belong in such a sacred place. Your garden has been carefully planted, deeply thought out and the Creator walks and lives within it. Allow Jesus to take control of your garden. You will need His help to get those rotten apples out. In fact, it's impossible to get such apples out on your own. The task is too big for your fragile human heart.

We were created to *need* the Lord. There is a strength found only in Christ, forgiveness found only with Christ, resilience found only in Christ. There are some apples within you that Christ needs to clean away. They are too heavy a burden for you to do on your own. The anger, the hurt, and the pain that these rotten apples have within you are excruciating. Your soul slowly cripples away as these rotten apples begin to ruin the freshly kept grass within your garden. The flowers you planted will be washed away with rotten apples. If you do not allow the Father to help you throw them over the fence, your garden will wither away. You need to humble yourself before the Lord and allow Him to work in your heart. These heavy burdens cannot be overcome alone. Reach out to the maker of your garden. Let Him move. You will see incredible things happen when you allow the Father to tend to your garden. Your heart will be transformed. Gorgeous flowers, trees, and plants will grow as Jesus plants new life, new thoughts, and new treasures within the garden of your heart. Trust Him and let go of these burdens, the apple tree in your garden may be picturesque, but it has the potential to produce destructive rotten apples that can rip your entire garden away. Be careful, be mindful and trust your Father for He cares for you.

"Humble yourselves, therefore, under the mighty hand of God so that at the proper time He may exalt you, casting all your anxieties on Him, because he cares for you".
(*NLT*, 1996, 1 Peter 5:6-7).

**CHAPTER THREE**

THE POND

One cold winters evening during my childhood, my family received an invitation to my Sunday School teacher's wedding. The invitation showed it would be a child-friendly event as there were outdoor games, a bouncy castle, and music planned for the children to dance to. I was already dreaming of the wedding, I could not wait for the big day to arrive. Only being ten years old, my young heart adored weddings as the brides looked like princesses, in my eyes. I used to draw what I guessed the wedding dress would look like before the big day and see if my prediction was right. Weddings were such a time of joy and happiness.

The weekend before the wedding, my mother took my sister Jayne and me into town to get new dresses. Jayne got a lovely blue dress with a matching silk scarf. I chose a dark pink dress with a white cardigan. As we were about to leave the shop, I noticed a pink headband that had diamonds on it. This headband caught my eye as it looked like a princess crown. When I was a child, this was an absolute dream. In my mind, I was a princess. Not a princess that demands her way, but a princess that knows her worth was found in her King, Jesus. A princess was a servant and that was her true crowning moment when she served those around her. Her greatest role model was her father, the King of Kings.

My mother saw me looking at the headband and decided to do something special for me.

"Amelia, would you and Jayne go grab my grocery list from the car? I need to pick up one more thing." She said with a cheeky grin on her face. Jayne and I strolled back to the car, just outside the shop. We put the new dresses and cardigans in the car and searched for my mother's list. Once we found it we walked back to the shop. As I walked towards my mother, I saw she had her hands behind her back.

"Close your eyes." She said with a smile.

As I closed them, I wished and hoped it was either the headband or a cookie from *Millie's Cookies Store*. That cookie store was my favorite. As I opened my eyes, she held up the princess crown and said I could wear it to the wedding. My heart sang as I put it straight onto my head and danced around the shop for a moment in joy. I thanked my mother many times for buying me the crown. I asked her how she knew I wanted it, she said it was the way my eyes lit up when I saw it. She knew it was something I would cherish.

Do you know that you are a child of God? Are you living out the life God has for you? He loves you unconditionally and has called you to live an abundant life, filled with purpose. You are royalty, you are special, you are precious and adored. My friend, you are fearfully and wonderfully made. The most precious gift to the Father is His children. He adores you and pursues you with great love, like no other. Stand up, you are royalty. Go and live your life in confidence for the King of Kings stands by you. He always looks for ways to brighten your day. Whether it be a strong eagle soaring through the sky or a radiant flower blooming on the first day of spring. Whatever makes your heart sing, notice the hidden miracles within each day. They are there, they are from the King. He longs to see you smile and dance for joy. He longs to hear you sing His name, as He adores you more than you know. Thank Him every day even for the little things. For there are so many wonderful reasons to praise the Lord.

When the day of the wedding finally arrived, Jayne and I couldn't wait to see the entertainment. When we first walked in, we took a seat and opened up the run sheet to see what the day would bring. The two things I loved most about weddings were seeing the bride walk down the aisle and taking note of her dress while flicking my eyes back to the groom and seeing how happy he was to see her. The other thing I loved most was the worship songs we would sing. When I checked the program, I saw they had a song about God's *Amazing Grace,* which made me even more excited.

Looking back, I didn't quite understand the notion of *Grace*. As a child, it meant Jesus forgave me and loved me even though I made mistakes. Now as an adult, I realize it goes deeper than this. Deep within my soul, I feel overwhelmed that the Lord would have mercy on me. I am a sinner and I am far from perfect, but the Lord still loves me and died for me. I was supposed to die on the cross because the price for my sinful choices, is death. Yet Christ died and let me live. I can walk in freedom now because of *Grace.* How precious is the love of Christ? He loves you that much, He is willing to cover the cost of our wrongdoings. This brings me to a new place of hope, restoration, and joy as I realize the heart of Christ is so good. Christ is loving, gracious, and kind. He died for you, walk in this new freedom. Walk through your *Garden of Grace.*

As we sat, music began to play and we were invited to stand. The bridesmaids slowly trickled down the aisle. One by one, each radiated joy and delight for their friend or family member who was getting married. Finally, the angelic bride arrived. Her dress reminded me of a princess. She looked exactly as I pictured, she was a real-life princess in my eyes. As she gently floated down the aisle, my eyes wandered back to her husband. He had tears pouring down his face in a beautiful, pure love moment. It almost made me want to cry it was such a precious experience.

God looks at you the way the man in the story looked at his new wife. Jesus says that He loves the church as if it were His bride because He laid His life down for the church. He loves you and everyone in the world with sacrificial love. This is an overwhelming love that every little girl should also dream about because they already have the greatest love story unfolding for them. The more you invest in your relationship and love for the Lord, the more love your heart will be filled with. When Jesus lives within your heart, your relationships with others can improve as you are able to show sacrificial love to those around you. We should all strive to love the Lord with all our hearts, all our minds, and with all our strengths.

> "You must love the Lord your God with all your heart, all your soul, and all your mind. This is the first and greatest commandment. A second is equally important: Love your neighbor as yourself."
>
> (*NLT*, 1996, Matthew 22:36-40).

From the moment you were knitted in your mother's womb, the Father loved you deeply. He continues to show this love all throughout your life. It is precious and wonderful to dream of such love from a husband. But remember that Christ loves you in a way that you cannot measure or know. The love of Christ is so treasurable and overwhelming.

The ceremony commenced and we sang the worship song, the vows took place, and James kissed his bride and they went to the garden to get photos. My sister Jayne and I were holding out for the children's entertainment that we were promised. As we walked around the back of the church to the garden, there it was- the bouncy castle, the outdoor games, and the most romantic pond I had ever seen. It was surrounded by wildflowers and luscious green grass. We started bouncing on the bouncy castle, then we moved to the lawn games and sweets table. The wedding was a child's dream. As we ran around, played games, and made new friends, our hearts were joyful. Jayne and I's new friends' names were Joseph and Lucy. Joseph was small with brown hair and bright brown eyes. He was wearing a navy blue suit and looked adorable. Joseph was about seven-years-old. Lucy was my age and she also had thick brown hair. She wore a pretty floral dress and looked like an angel.

The four of us decided to head over to the romantic pond. This pond was quite small, but it seemed to be very deep. We were walking around the edge singing a song to each other. Playing the game, *don't step on a crack.* Which meant we couldn't step on the cracks of the tiles around the pond. If you did, then you were out. Round and round we went, singing, laughing, and playing. We were a little further away from the other children. The adults were in sight, but far away from us. Jayne and Joseph were walking in front of me.

Blissfully we played, laughed, and sang songs around the pond. I started to notice how slippery the tiles were getting as Lucy splashed droplets of water onto us. It was all fun and games until I almost slipped over. I started to think that we probably shouldn't be skipping around a slippery pond. But before I could say something, Joseph stepped on a crack in the tiles and slipped hard into the pond. With a big splash and thud, I saw Joseph hit his head on the tiles before landing into the deep, dark water. Joseph began to sink into the hidden pond. He didn't come up for a few moments, we shouted and reached for him but we couldn't find him. Lucy ran towards the adults screaming that Joseph had fallen into the pond. Little

Joseph couldn't swim, especially since this was a winter wedding and the water would have been freezing. He hit his head too, so we weren't sure if he was conscious. Jayne bravely jumped into the water to save Joseph.

With a splash, her new turquoise dress was drenched in pond water. She dived down under the ice-cold water. When she came up for a breathe, you could see the fear in her eyes as she was not sure if she could save Joseph. Finally, she felt his arm and pulled with all her strength to bring him to the surface of the water. Once his head reached the surface of the water, I reached my hand down to help bring him back out of the pond. Together, we pulled and pushed and grunted as we struggled to get him out of the water. As my hands touched his arm, I felt how cold his body had gotten.

I began to worry that he was unconscious. With a thud, Joseph was out of the water and safely on the tiles. I could see his head had a bruise and blood dripped down his soft cheek. I grabbed ahold of him and held his head up and tried to get him to wake up. I looked up and saw his father had reached us. Terror and shock filled his eyes. He sat down next to me and I moved back to give him room. He continuously thanked Jayne and me for helping get his son out of the pond. Joseph's mother had called the ambulance and quickly Joseph was taken to hospital. The doctors said that if it wasn't for my sister Jayne, the sweet boy would have died that day.

My sister Jayne, was brave, determined, and never gave up. She had a spirit that fought for what she believed in and when someone was in trouble, she would do all that she could to help them. She saved that little boy's life. To thank Jayne for her noble act, the family bought her a beautiful lilac angel that hung above her bed each night. The family said that Jayne will forever be their angel, for bringing their Joseph out of the pond. This was a story of a great rescue.

Take a moment to think about your life. Have there ever been moments when you have suddenly been taken away from something or someone? A sudden job loss, a relationship ending, or needing to move house? I have experienced times where I thought I was in the right situation, yet God needed to rescue me and bring me out. It was only when I was out of the situation and looked back, that I realized, I have not broken apart or ripped away from something that was going to benefit me, but in fact, I was rescued from something that may have harmed me.

God is our great rescuer and He will close doors when the time is right. When this happens, you need to calmly and gracefully walk away. Trust that God rescued you for a reason and there is something better for you ahead. You may feel like the boy in the pond sometimes. Overwhelmed by what is happening to you. Struggling to breathe and make it back to the surface of the water. Slowly, you reach out to God as He rescues you. Gently your hero saves you from the harmful mess you got yourself into and He recovers you. Your heart will need time to heal and your wounds may leave a scar, but the Lord has rescued you from something that was not intended for you.

Have faith my friend, trust in God. His timing is perfect,

His plan for you is far greater than what you could have imagined. I believe you are where you are for a reason and for a purpose. Keep talking with God and listening to where He is guiding your next steps. Things may turn out differently from how you planned, but believe me, when I say, God has bigger and brighter plans for your future. You may be looking at the past hurt and blaming God, but have you ever thought to thank Him? This may have just been one big great rescue for you. Trust Him, He has great things coming your way. You are brave and strong. You have the ability to walk away from closed doors. Do not sit at the door waiting for it to open, you may see a glimpse of the door open again. Be careful to not reach inside at this point, as the door may slam back at you and harm you even more than when you first were taken out. Courageously walk away. You are filled with strength and dignity. Hold your head high. Straighten your crown and know that the King of Kings will look after your next steps. Walk away, there are better things ahead. Trust in the Lord's timing for His ways are higher than our own.

**CHAPTER FOUR**
THE RABBIT

My local Primary school was small, bright, and beautiful. Everyone in the village knew all the teachers and every student was part of one family. There was an essence of community within this school, everyone belonged. As a Primary teacher now, I look back and realize how wonderful this school was. They were inclusive and their classrooms were filled with colors and life. The one thing that stood out to me the most was my two friends, Bethany and Esther. Bethany had shining blonde hair that fell just below her shoulders. Her smile would light up a room and her laugh was contagious. To this day, I have not met anyone with such a gentle spirit as beautiful Bethany. Esther was strong, brave, and an adventure friend. She would always initiate our adventures and come up with wonderful ideas of how we could spend our weekends. She had gorgeous brown hair that was just slightly shorter than Bethany's. Esther had a fringe that brushed across her eyebrows and in the summertime, it would fall down past her eyes and the wind would blow it across her face, making it hard for her to see sometimes. Our recess times were filled with wonderful imaginative games. Many of our games were about pretending to be animals. Bethany and Esther adored cats and would always pretend we were playful, fluffy cats roaming the beautiful British field in which we played in.

Cats were not an animal I looked for affection from, Yet, I still found myself participating in the adventurous cat games with Bethany and Esther. An animal that caught my eye one day when I was at Esther's house was a striking, sweet bunny rabbit. Esther had two pure white rabbits that had just had baby rabbits. My heart was filled with so much joy. As I held one of these rabbits in the palm of my hand I knew that rabbits were the animal for me. There was one in particular that stood out to me. He was playful, delicate, and kept coming closer to me. We shared a connection that day and all I could think about when I got home was asking my parents if we could have a rabbit one day. As I waved goodbye to Esther and her mother after they dropped me back at my house from our playdate, I rehearsed in my mind how I could convince my parents we needed a rabbit. Over and over the lines ran through my mind, *Please can we have a rabbit? I will take full responsibility for this rabbit and will feed them every day.*

Working up the courage, I walked into my sweet British home and saw my mother cooking us spaghetti for dinner.

My mouth began to water as I thought about how delicious dinner was going to be. I needed to focus, switch back to my mission: convince my parents I needed a rabbit. Apprehensively, I walked into the kitchen to greet my mother with a smile.

"Amelia, did you enjoy going to Esther's house?" She said gently.

"Oh yes! And you will never guess, her rabbits had babies and I got to look at the baby bunnies and I love them so much. They were so soft and small." I said with great enthusiasm.

"That sounds nice." Said my mother with a smile.

"I was wondering if we could maybe ask Esther's mum if we could have one of her baby rabbits? I think we need a rabbit and I would look after them and feed them. Oh please mum, please!" I begged.

I began to get a little too excited at this idea. Once the words came from my mouth I realized how silly my idea was, my mother would never agree to a new animal with such short notice. Esther's family was giving the rabbits away the following week, I had left it too late. My excitement began to dimmer as I waited for my mother's response. A moment of silence occurred while she stirred the mince for our spaghetti. More silence followed. Then the words that brought my innocent childhood world into a state of pure joy were spoken,

"A rabbit sounds nice, I'll call Esther's mum tomorrow." Said my mother, with a slight grin on her face.

"Wait, we are getting a rabbit?" My voice got louder and my heart filled with joy.

"Well, let me check with dad, but I know he would love this idea." She sounded so certain. This was really happening.

The next day my dad woke me up for school and told me that after school we were going shopping for our new rabbits' things. Once I got to school, I ran into the playground as fast as I could.

"Esther! Esther! Did you hear? We are keeping one of your rabbits!" I yelled across the playground. The whole of the village would have heard the great news, that's how loud my voice got at this moment. The day at school could not have taken any longer, I watched the clock till it was time for dad to take me to get my new rabbit products. As soon as 3 pm came, I raced off to my hook and grabbed my bookbag. Pushing past the tall Year 6's I raced to see my dad's car in the car park and jumped into his car as fast as I could.

We went to the pet store to get food, a hutch, a little rabbit bed, a water jug, a brush, and anything else we could think of. This was one of those days that sticks with you forever. A day that you look back on and can feel the joy you felt in that moment. The new rabbit was set to arrive the following Saturday and my heart was overflowing with happiness. Saturday arrived and I woke to a chilly morning. I looked over at my window and saw how frosty and cold it was outside. I jumped out of bed and my feet froze, it was an icy day today. Putting on my warmest clothes, I brushed my hair into a high ponytail. I liked the way my wavy brown hair would tickle the back of my neck when I wore my hair that way. Looking at the mirror, I smiled as it was the day I would become a rabbit owner. Looking into my reflection's eyes, I smiled and reminded myself how I needed to be a strong, brave carer for my new rabbit. I smiled at the thought of my rabbit and quickly ran to the car to meet dad.

Together, my father and I drove to Esther's house. On the drive, I began brainstorming names for my new friend. As I looked out at the cloudy sky, I noticed something magical began to happen. The sky let out sprinkles of snow. As we kept driving, the snow picked up and started landing on the ground softly. I noticed the snow landing on the roofs of the village houses. It also landed on the leaves in the trees then slowly trickled back down to the ground. The snow fell so tenderly, it reminded me of the magical land of *Narnia*. We arrived at Esther's house and I could see my new rabbit was there waiting for me. I ran over to him and held him in my arms. As I brushed his soft fur against my face, I looked up at the snow, I knew what this little rabbit's name would be.

"Snowy, I'll call him Snowy," I said with a content heart. From that day onwards, Snowy was my priority. I taught him to come when I called his name, he would sit for me and lay down when I asked. I fed him more than enough food and even took him to do laps around the garden to keep up his health. When friends came over, they would hold my Snowy and tell me how well trained he was. I was so proud of my little guy. I trained him to be gentle, kind, and sweet to those around him. He never bit or scratched anyone. He soon became a house rabbit, so I set up a little bed and toilet for him in our dining room. He was the most well-behaved rabbit. When I came home from school, Snowy would run to the door and we would play and cuddle. The only treats he loved more than carrots, were green beans. Every week we would have to stock up on extra green beans for Snowy. Another thing I taught him, was to come when I called the word *beans*. It did not matter where he was in the house, he would come when I said,

"Snow, Snow, bean beans."

I would rustle the bean packet and moments later, my Snowy would run to me with great excitement. He ate more beans than I did. He was healthy, strong, and the most loyal rabbit. It did not matter what he did, I would love him unconditionally.

The notion of unconditional love is the love Christ has for you. At the age of ten, I began to realize, that no matter what, Jesus really did love us deeply. When I look back and think about the excitement I had when Snowy would come to me, this was just a glimpse into the excitement God has when you reach out to Him. He waits, patiently for His children to come back into His arms. No matter what you have done, or where you have been, Jesus loves you more than you could ever imagine. Jesus died for you, that is the greatest love story you will ever hear. The love story of you and Christ. A love that is unconditional and never-ending.

**CHAPTER FIVE**
THE SUNDAY

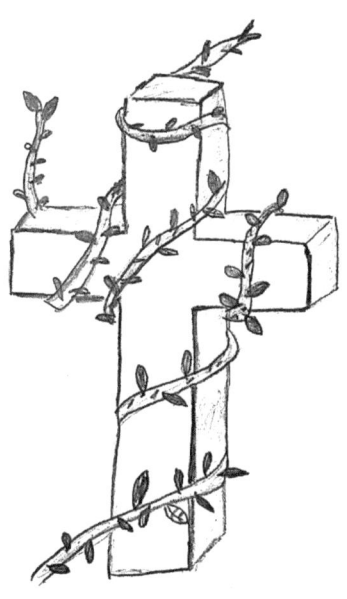

Grief is a pain that cripples your heart and suffocates your soul. A pain that takes you to a different place. A location where only God can reach you. An unfathomable, gloomy, lonely place. God sits with you here, while you journey through your suffering and confusion.

Your heart aches for the one who you cannot see. Softly you whisper to Heaven, hoping they are alright. Anger furies within as you try to understand why such a tragedy could happen. Especially to someone so gentle and kind. You question where God is. You wonder if He is still in control. Faith is all you have left. Yet it is exactly what tears you apart. For you do not know what the future will hold. So, in Faith, you trust that the Lord will carry you safely home one day. With all that is within you, you pray, you hope and you persevere.

One Sunday morning I woke to the sound of worship music in the kitchen. My mother was doing her morning devotion while my father and sister were getting ready for church. My parents were the Pastors of our church and Sundays were always church days for us. I quickly washed my face and headed downstairs to eat my cereal at the table while I listened quietly to the peaceful worship music. I looked out the window and saw the blossoms blooming out on the tree branches. It was starting to transition into spring, which meant I was able to wear a dress to church that week.

Heading up to my room I found a pretty pink dress with a white cardigan that had brown buttons on it. To match, I also put on white fluffy tights and white shoes that had little bows on them. I brushed my hair softly and asked my mother to put it into a bun. Wearing my hair this way made me feel elegant and like a true ballerina. Once I was ready for church I went to the fridge and called out,

"Snow, Snow, bean beans"

Quickly my little man raced to the fridge where I gave him a large handful of beans. He was a happy bunny. With no one looking, I gave him one more handful to make sure he was full while we were at church. This was around the same time that we had just gotten our new puppy, George. He was energetic, cute but very cheeky. He had black and white fur and floppy ears. His left ear had a big patch of white on it, this was what made him unique in his litter, he did not look like any of the others.

This memory of playing with George as a puppy and Snowy as a fully grown, fluffy bunny made my heart sing. It was one of those moments that you treasure deep within your soul. I was a young, innocent child enjoying the first day of spring in my pink dress and ballerina bun. Smelling the flowers and dancing through the garden. Jesus was in that garden with me, as my heart was filled with bliss, God loves to see His children's hearts sing praises of joy for Him.

God longs for all of His children to live in such freedom and joy each and every day of their lives. That was why He died on the cross for us, to save us. We walk in freedom now because of Him and can dance and sing praises of joy for the Lord is good.

As my mother called me inside to go to church that warm spring morning, I checked the gates were closed, and Snowy and George were happy with lots of water and carrots. I held my Snowy tight and gave him my final cuddle. I felt the soft fluff on his back brush against my rosy cheeks and it tickled me a little, making me giggle. With a kiss on his head and a hug goodbye, I put my Snowy down and waved to the puppy and bunny.

The service was wonderful and challenging. I was in the Sunday School program and enjoyed learning about the fruits of the spirit. These included,

"Love, joy, peace, patience, kindness, goodness, faithfulness, gentleness, and self-control. There is no law against these things."

(*NLT, 1996,* Galatians 5:22-23).

We went and got lunch in town afterward. My mother had a tradition, where we would go to Tesco's to get groceries then pick up a Krispy Kreme donut while we were there. As I sat in the car eating my donut with my sticky fingers, I gazed out the window and thought of my morning with Snowy and George. As we walked in the door, my sister said we should go jump on the trampoline, but we needed to change out of our church clothes first. I quickly went upstairs and put on a white shirt that had a picture of a horse on the front and my blue denim shorts. Calling down the hallway I said,

"I'll meet you outside when you're ready"

"Okay, I'm just finding my shorts, I'll be down in a minute." She replied.

Peacefully I walked downstairs in my slipper socks. I chose to walk through the kitchen so I could slide across the tiles on my way through to the back door. Putting on my shoes, I noticed George and Snowy weren't anywhere to be seen. As I opened the back door, the fresh spring air brushed against my skin and the air smelled of a Sunday Barbeque. My neighbor Eden was jumping on her trampoline, so I waved and told her she should come over to my house to play with my sister and I.

"Let me go ask mum, I'll be out in a minute." Said Eden.

As I waited for Eden and my sister Jayne, I searched

the garden for Snowy and George. I began calling out their names, but I couldn't find them. Suddenly, I saw little George slowly walking towards me from around the corner of the house, near our garden shed. He was covered in blood. His head was down in shame.

My eyes fill with tears for my new puppy. *Was he hurt? Had a fox gotten in and attacked him?* I thought.

Rapidly, I ran around the corner of the house to comfort my sweet puppy when my world was shattered.

There, lying next to the garden shed was Snowy. My dear, sweet Snowy whom I had loved for the past few years, was lying there, no longer alive. He was covered in blood and I could see he wasn't breathing anymore. His tail was missing and he had bite marks on him. Standing there, frozen in time. My world was broken down for the first time, there had been a loss in my life, but this hit me on a personal level. The shock overwhelmed me and I began to sob.

Hastily I walked back inside to find Jayne. Looking around the house, I couldn't see anyone. I knew my father was out for a meeting, so I went upstairs to my mother's room. When I arrived my sister Jayne and my mother were sitting on my mother's bed talking.

"Sorry, I was just about to come down, mum and I were just talking, what happened?" Said Jayne, with compassion in her eyes.

"It's Snowy, he's been hurt," I replied.

Together we went downstairs, my neighbor Eden joined us as we all walked into the garden together. My mother brought a towel to wrap Snowy in. She picked him up and with tears in her eyes, she shook her head.

"He's gone." She said.

Even within the garden of our hearts, hurt, pain and grief can come. This type of pain has the power to ruin your beautiful garden if you allow it to. It's in these times that we need to stay strong and hold close to our Heavenly Father. While my childhood grief was only for a bunny rabbit, I believe God used this story to strengthen my heart for the future.

Little did I know, there would be even greater grief that was to come my way when I was sixteen and I needed this area of my heart to have strength. Trust your heart, for God made it. While you may be feeling deep pain right now, the Father is reaching out to you ever so gently. Softly, He extends His hand towards you. He longs to comfort you and bless you. He cries with you. All those nights you poured out your soul's pain, Jesus was listening.

Give your deepest pains to Him. Allow Him to move in your life. Let Him touch your heart. Listen to your heart, those whispers you heard from God, they were for you. Listen, trust and believe that God will get you through this. He is the gardener of your heart, allow Him to restore you. Let Him in again, open the gates to your garden, allow Him to move you to a new place, a stronger and brighter place. Give the key to your heart back to the Creator. He will restore you.

> "Create in me a clean heart, O God. Renew a loyal

spirit within me. Do not banish me from your presence, and don't take your Holy Spirit from me."

(*NLT,* 1996, Psalms 51:10-11).

**CHAPTER SIX**
THE ANGEL

Years passed by and I had moved to Australia. My family moved across the world to run a church. Sixteen- years old, my heart had faced some life-changing experiences, yet there were many more to come. The school I attended was a welcoming Christian School that was just down the road from my house. Jayne also went to the same school and we had a great community of friends around us. While we were no longer in a village, our city had a country feel to it. There was a big hill just behind our house and we would take George on walks up there. Our George was most definitely forgiven for the hurt he caused me all those years ago. We brought him over to Australia with us and he enjoyed his time in the hot country of Australia. Although, the vets would say he was,

"Allergic to Australia." The grass gave him rashes, the air made him sneeze and the big hills behind our house gave him arthritis. Living in two countries for a dog was quite an achievement, but for George, Australia was not the desired country to move to. While living a life full of allergies and sore muscles, he loved to run across the sweltering grass and swim in the creeks.

I was a competitive swimmer when I lived in Australia. Swimming ran in the family, my great grandfather, my grandparents, uncles, and father all competed in swimming. My Uncle Brett held the records and was the fastest breaststroker in the region. My father used to tell me my gift and passion for swimming came from Uncle Brett. My dear Uncle is in Heaven now, but I know he is watching over me and I hoped my swimming success made him and my family proud.

Every morning and evening my father would drive me to train for two hours. The sessions averaged 6km, so around 12km of swimming a day. There were also gym sessions twice a week as well as runs around the local lake. Swimming was my world, it was my passion. My days were filled with pain, suffering, and determination as I swam hard every session. Most nights I would go to bed with sore muscle, wet hair, and smelling like chlorine. It was an incredible way of dealing with stress and anxiety as my swimming days were during high school. There was always a lot on my mind, from school dramas to assignments, I had a lot to think about as I swam back and forth, over and over again. The physical aching pains I felt in my body when I pushed myself past my breaking point, were what grew me into the person I am today. This season of life taught me to be resilient. To always push through, even when it seemed impossible. I became strong through my swimming season.

The day I met Elizabeth, my world changed. We were only eleven years old, yet our young hearts clicked. She was brave, strong-willed, determined and an inspiration to me. We were sitting in the marshaling rows before we competed in the 100m Breaststroke when I first met her. I looked over and said to the brave girl with the curly hair,

"Hey, I think these are your googles, I found them on the floor."

"Oh, thanks. I'm Elizabeth." She said with a confident smile on her face. She inspired me, she was so self-assured. We were about to race in a big Sydney interstate competition and this was my first time attending such a large-scale competition. I was completely shaking sitting there on those cold white chairs. In rows we sat, waiting for our names to be called. With all the pressure on us to succeed, I wondered how she could just sit there with a calm, smile on her face. Who was this girl? How was she so brave? Right as I was about to reply, my race got called to go.

"I'm Amelia, Good luck in your race Elizabeth!" I called to her as I walked towards my race. My heart began to race. I could feel the beats pounding against my chest. *Please Lord, calm my heart for I am terrified.* I took a deep breath and walked towards the blocks. Looking up, the lights were bright, the room was loud. My mind went blank and all I could focus on was the race. The whistle blew, it was time to stand on the blocks. I always held my breath in these moments, to calm my shakes.

"Take your marks, Go!" The man in white would say.

Off I went, I swam as hard as I could. As I did my final kicks and reached the wall, I looked up at my time and was shocked, I had gone faster than I ever had before. The first thing I looked for at that moment was the smiles on my family's faces. The proud look my father gave me made all the early morning training sessions worth it. That moment, that feeling, was what I lived for.

After I stayed back and watched Elizabeth's race. She did even better than me, I was so happy for her. I waited for her to hop out of the water to congratulate her. She looked up and saw me,

"Hey, good job in your race, I saw your time!" She said.

"Thanks, Elizabeth, you did amazing, look at your time! You made the finals, congratulations!" I replied.

I was truly happy for my brave new friend. Later I invited her to share my lollies with me and we went to the cool-down pool together. From that day onwards, she was one of the first people I would look for at the pool when I arrived for competitions. A few years down the track, we ended up buying matching swimmers and would always take photos together matching and shining with joy.

After many years of swim camps, life chats, and jokes, she was filled with laughter and delight, my lovely Elizabeth.

One day, when I was sixteen, I went to a competition and the day was just like any other day. Racing, laughing, seeing my friends but most of all, I spent time with Elizabeth. I remember this particular day, I ate a Carmel donut. It was the best I had ever had and it made my day a lot brighter. Now when I eat Carmel donuts I am reminded of that day.

As the competition came to an end, I went to find Elizabeth to take a photo together as we always did at our competitions. As I gave her a hug goodbye after the photos and walked in the opposite direction, my innocent heart had no idea this would be the last time I would ever see my brave friend. That photo was my final memory of our friendship. The memory of walking away from her runs through my mind all the time. I remember looking over my shoulder and giving her one last wave as I walked out the door. I longed to go back into that final moment, to give her one last hug, to tell her one last time that I loved her.

Some time had passed by and I hadn't heard from Elizabeth. I finally got a phone call explaining her absence. Sitting on the end of my bed with a muesli bar in my hand. I was about to go to afternoon training. I was told, my brave curly-haired friend had passed on. There had been a tragic car accident and she was hit by a car while crossing the road. The doctors did all they could, but she was in Heaven now.

My body went into shock, I was frozen for a moment as my mind tried to comprehend the news I had just heard. I picked up my pillow and my body collapsed to the floor in disbelief. I lay on the floor and sobbed my heart out. I felt the carpet underneath me began to soak up my tears. I cried out to God, I needed Him in that moment, I needed someone. I felt so broken. After I worked up the courage to stand up, all I could do was walk downstairs and see who was home. My other sister Sarah was sitting on the couch. As soon as I saw her, I broke down into tears again. Sarah did all she could to comfort me, but she didn't even know what had happened as I couldn't form words.

Soon my father came home to drive me to swim training. He heard the news and asked if I wanted to stay home instead. I told him, I needed to go, for Elizabeth. As I arrived, everyone saw me and ran to me for a warm embrace. In a big group, we all began to cry. I had never experienced anything like this. People crying for me and with me. This was a community of support. Those closest to Elizabeth sat in a circle around the Tuggeranong pool and shared their favorite memories of Elizabeth. While this was a beautiful moment, it was the hardest and most devastating moment I had to endure. Re-living old memories of someone who had recently passed was a pain I had not yet experienced. Yet, it brought comfort, as I felt closer to my friend in Heaven.

The next four days the grief and shock really settled into my heart. I stayed in my room and only left to go to the bathroom and to have baths. My mother would bring food, tea, and water up to me. One thing I will always remember was the fluffy Pj's my mother bought me during this time. They were the sort of pajamas that felt like you were being wrapped in a fluffy blanket. During my dark days, I wrote everything in a journal, drew pictures, and painted. I wrote letters to God and gave Him my pain and depression. This was the only way out of such a dark, endless place. Continuously I would pray. How my heart hurt and longed to see my friend just one last time. I printed a picture of Elizabeth and placed it in my prayer corner to always lift her and her family up in prayer. I also faced Glandular fever during this time, which led to chronic fatigue. The depression and dark mindset I went into made my recovery slower and harder to fight. I ended up quitting swimming due to my chronic fatigue, but also the depression I fell into from the loss of my friend. I gave myself a year to recover physically and mentally. While this time was hard, it grew me into the person I am today.

Here is my prayer for you during your time of grief:

Dear Heavenly Father,
Comfort, restore, and heal me. I need you to come into my heart and rescue me from this pain. Guide me on my journey of grief, help me to seek you for comfort.
Thank you for your promises, thank you for your Word. Help me through this tough time.
In Jesus Name,
Amen.

My journey of grieving looks different from yours. We all experience pain and loss in our own ways. One thing I learned was that it was good and healthy to feel the pain. I encourage you to allow yourself to feel the full extent of the pain if you are in a safe, well-supported place in your life. It is when your mind feels ready to face the pain of the past that you can really begin to heal.

Your heartbreak is just like any other injury, you need to feel the pain to make it through the journey of healing. Allow yourself to feel in the quiet moments. Pushing these feelings away for too long can lead to problems later on in life. *Let your heart feel, let your heart heal.*

Pray every day, write letters to God, be honest with your Father for He cares deeply for you. Give Him your deepest pains, hurts, and desires. Allow Him to comfort you during these dark times. Just remember that joy does come again. Joy is just around the corner, stay hopeful and faithful, for the Lord your God is with you.

*For my sweet Elizabeth in Heaven, I whisper a gentle prayer to Heaven and hope that you know how loved, cherished, and adored you are down here. Our friendship was something I shall forever hold within my heart. God bless your beautiful family.*

"Yet what we suffer now is nothing compared to the glory he will reveal to us later."

(*NLT*, 1996, Romans 8:18).

**CHAPTER SEVEN**

THE KEY

The garden of your heart is precious and sacred. There is a beautiful white fence that surrounds it. This fence is your protection wall to set healthy boundaries. Every garden has a key, a gate, and a choice. You have the choice about whether you keep your gate open to all, or if you set up a protection wall. This stops people from entering your beautiful garden if their intention is to harm you. It is important that with this analogy, you know there is a healthy balance that we all need to strive and find. The Bible teaches us to *guard our hearts,*

> "Guard your heart above all else, for it determines the course of your life"

(*NLT,* 1996, Proverbs 4:23).

Boundaries are the first step to creating healthy relationships with those around you. This is a great way to set limits for how much you invest, or receive from relationships. It also allows you to stand firm on your morals, values, and beliefs. Assertiveness can be achieved through a gentle and kind spirit. This means, be kind with your words towards others, yet being straightforward and clear of your boundaries as you speak. I encourage you to stand strong in who you are and know yourself before you give too much of yourself away to those around you.

Your identity is a key part of knowing your strengths, limits, and who you are in Christ. Stay true to who you are and know that you are enough. Think back to my garden story in chapter one, this notion of being *good enough* was a mindset, we are all good enough because we are all children of God. Knowing your worth and staying true to who you are, is a key factor in having healthy relationships. Allow yourself to grow, yet keep the core of your identity found in Christ.

Many times over I have seen people within the church giving from a generous servant's heart. Unfortunately, they had burnout and lost interest in serving within the church.

When you give too much of your heart's flowers away, your garden begins to dry up and the flowers within your heart are no longer there. This is because you neglect to water your own garden as well as others. While this is honorable, it is important to be mindful that you cannot sustain this if you are not looking after yourself as well. Your flowers are no longer within your garden, they are with everyone else as you have given so much away. You need to make sure that when you give, you also receive from Christ. This way, your garden will always be full of flowers to give, for the Lord will strengthen you and keep you, to make sure you can continue to serve. This is not the same as giving and expecting to receive. This is about investing in Christ as you give to others as you will see that your garden needs refreshing every so often, as all people's gardens do. We cannot do everything in our own strength, we need the strength of the Father to keep us going. As you give and as you serve make sure you set up your boundaries and take care of yourself as well. This way you can give wholeheartedly as your garden will never run dry of water to give or flowers to bless.

Another aspect of your heart is supporting others. When I was a youth leader and girls Bible study mentor, I experienced many times when my young girls would come to me seeking wisdom and Godly counsel. In these moments, I would need to pray that the Lord would answer and guide these girls through my words. I would pray:

*May my words be silenced as the Holy Spirit speaks through me.*

This was important to guard my heart because as a leader, it could be very difficult to set boundaries when you have so much love and compassion for your teens within the youth ministry. Allow the Holy Spirit to guide you and let Him help you as you take on the burdens of others. I walked the journey of some very heavy stories that made my heart feel burdened. The only way I could be there as a support for these girls was to give these to the Holy Spirit and let Him lead the way.

My human heart could not take on the weight of the

world, yet the Lord can. Christ died on the cross carrying all of our sins. He is strong, we need Him to make it through and to keep our gardens growing healthy and strong. The gate to your garden is an important aspect to think about. It is a gate, so it has the ability to be opened or closed at any given time. Some people live under the illusion that others have the power over the gate, but in reality, you have the choice to open it or close it. This links to the notion of not being able to control what others do or say but having control over how you react.

If someone hurts you, deep within your core. You may wait and see if they will come back through your gate. You do all you can, you pray, you reach out but nothing seems to be working. For some reason, you cannot control this person's behavior. Have you ever found yourself in a situation where you are convinced you have control over the entire scenario? Well, unfortunately, this is not how the garden of your heart works. In fact, you only have control over how you respond or behave. So when someone does something hurtful or wrong to you, it is wise to give the situation to Christ. Ask Him for guidance on how you can approach the situation. You cannot plan how they will react, you cannot force them to re-enter your garden either. If their time in your heart has passed, and they are walking away, you need to caringly leave them a bunch of your flowers and close the gate to your heart from them. Set this boundary for your own protection. If they hurt you and choose to walk away, you do not need to fight them or convince them to stay. All you need to do is graciously and kindly say, *thank you for the time you spent in my garden and goodbye.*

Gently close the gate and continue to tend to your own garden with the Lord. Forgive this person for your own garden's sake and give everything else to the Lord. Forgiveness may take you a few days, weeks, or years of gardening before you are ready. If the person who has just left your garden has actually taken parts of your garden with them and left the garden in a tragic state. Let them take it, walk away and let God refresh your garden to be brighter and even more abundant than before they came. God is outside of time and He already knew you were going to let this person into your heart. He knew they would take away parts of your identity and rip you of who you truly are. He knew that the Grace you once walked in, no longer applies as the person came right in and spread lies into your heart. God knew this would happen, it was no accident.

Do not feel shame for allowing this person in. However, God can turn all things into good and He has a beautiful plan for you.

The lies that these people feed into your garden grow like weeds, fast and uncontrollably. It is important that at first sight of weeds growing, you ask the Lord to help you remove them from your garden. If you do not, they will grow over the top of everything that was already there and your entire garden could soon become one big lie of weeds. This is a drastic analogy, yet I have experienced this at one point in time. One simple lie was spoken over my life. I allowed the garden gate to be opened to the person who spoke over me. The weed came in and my garden began to overflow with weeds. The one lie spoken over me was actually an endless spiral of lies that was connected to other areas of my garden. slowly I began to get confused between what was a weed and what was the true plants that the Lord had been growing in my heart. All those beautiful childhood rose bushes I once planted, were covered in weeds and my identity was a lie. Have you ever experienced this sort of pain? A pain where you are so lost and tangled within the lies, you no longer know right from wrong, truth from lie, forward from backward. You are entangled in the vines and are trapped within the lies of your own heart. It is an awful place to be and can lead people to dark places, as their hearts no longer reflect their true identity.

If you are in this place, I first encourage you to gently and kindly close the gate of your heart to the person speaking these lies over you. Then one by one, slowly and surely God will untangle you from the lies. This is a journey and a process and cannot always be fixed overnight. At first, you will get untangled, but the weeds will still be in your garden, leaving your heart in a jumble. There is still confusion between what is weed and what is not. So even when you begin to break free from these lies, they are still in the garden until you actively remove them. In time, you and the Lord can work through these weeds and remove them.

Once all the weeds are out, your garden will be a blank bed of soil and you need to replant truth back into your heart. This is an important phase, if you stop at this point, you will be vulnerable, able to accept the truth, or re-grow your garden with more lies again. Stay strong during this re-growth time. It can be a hard time to re-find your identity in Christ. I encourage you to trust the Lord and give Him your worries during this time. One thing to keep in mind is that the garden of your heart is a lifetime journey and there will always be weeds coming in and out of the garden. You will always need to tend to your garden. Over time your ability to know what is a weed and what is not will strengthen. In time, it will become easier to throw the weed out straight away, rather than allowing it to settle in your soil.

If you are still at a vulnerable point in your life, I encourage you to give the key back to Jesus. The key to your heart is His if you allow Him to have it. He will look after you and guard you against trouble. While this sounds simple, it is an ongoing process where every single day you need to make the decision to give Christ the key to your heart. Our vulnerable human minds sometimes need to take control of our own lives and we feel we know best for ourselves. God is saying to peacefully and calmly trust in Him. He created your heart, He knows who is best to come into the garden.

There are people who have wrong intentions and can actually destroy your garden if you allow them to. Remember that you have a lot of choices in this matter. Listen to where the Holy Spirit is guiding you. Give the key to Jesus and let Him be the keeper of your garden. While you wait for God to open the gate of your heart to someone, keep working on your heart. Each day, tend to it and plant new truths within your life. Continue to bless others and give flowers away, as long as you are being filled back up with Christ's love and strength.

You are so precious, take care of your garden.

**CHAPTER EIGHT**

THE WILLOW TREE

The willow of wonder, the willow of faith. The willow of pain that brings life again. My dear friend Isla has always shared admiration of willow trees with me. When we were young, we would have art days and use watercolors to paint wonderful, colorful pictures of willow trees.

Putting God first can be the most challenging aspect of your relationship with Him. Life can get really busy and overwhelming at times. Your children are having troubles at school, their washing has not been done, you need to drive them around to three different soccer ovals in one afternoon, the pantry is empty and the kids are hungry. You have three assignments due, working full time, yet still, need to find time to exercise and rest. How are you supposed to find a balance in such a busy lifestyle? How are you supposed to find time for God? He should be your first thought as you wake up. He should be on your mind all throughout your day and the last thought you have as you go to sleep at night. I challenge you to wake up tomorrow and say a prayer before your feet even hit the ground for the day. Talk to God about your to-do list, or your plans. Maybe it is time to slow your life down, reassess your priorities and rediscover a new way of doing life with Jesus. Slow down, set goals, and pray continually. God longs to hear from you.

Patiently He waits for your beautiful eyes to flutter open in the morning.

As your mind begins to tick off all the hard tasks you have set out for yourself, slow down at this moment and before you even allow your mind to race, pray. Before your feet touch the floor, pray. Before you leave the house and hop into the car, pray. Submit your day to God. Put Him first in all that you do and good things will flow from this. Let us go back to Genesis and the Garden of Eden. In the cool of the evening, the Lord would walk with His creation. Mankind was created in the image of God, first.

> "So God created human beings in his own image.
> In the image of God he created them;
> male and female he created them."
>
> (*NLT*, 1996, Genesis 1:27).

Adam and Eve saw themselves as failures, they saw themselves as worthless. Their desires to have wisdom beyond what they could handle, caused astronomical effects, as they no longer saw the value of themselves.

How you see yourself is highly important because it

determines the steps you take. If you see yourself as not worthy, not good enough, and not important, you will live by this. Your mind is a dangerous place, it has the ability to lead your heart towards great love or great hate. You need to understand that God, the creator of the universe designed you and loves you. While you were in your mother's womb, God planned your existence. He knows everything you think, speak or do even before you do it. He knows you more than you even know yourself. He planned your paths, He guides your steps. He is worthy of all praise for He has created such magnificent people.

You are beautiful, you are radiant, you are graceful, you are loved, and you are worthy. I hope you can begin to see that before you even achieve anything today, you are already amazing in the eyes of God. You are already worthy, you are already beautiful and you are already loved.

Beloved, you are more than enough, more than a conqueror. Hold your crown and your head high, for the King of Kings, has created an angelic, elegant princess. You are so worthy, smile my friend, for you have so many beautiful reasons to be grateful. While you were worthy before you even got out of bed this morning, remember that we were created to live an abundant and full life. The river of life can flow right through you and you can do wonderful things with this life. Oh, how precious are the thoughts God has about you. He just loves to pray for you and think of you. You are His most precious treasure. He longs for the best for you. That is why He has placed a desire in your heart to work hard and achieve your goals. Think back to the analogy of the garden, it does not just grow itself, it requires hard work. Daily tending to for the flowers to bloom, the grass to spring from the ground, and for the weeds to be trimmed. We are designed to create beauty, the way God has created beauty in you. His creation is mighty and wonderous, it is a system designed to need hard work for sustainability. The garden needs to be tended to, the garden needs hard work to shine. He has created the most beautiful sceneries for us to enjoy, but for us to have food, and survive, we must grow crops, harvest, and work.

> "Work willingly at whatever you do, as though you were working for the Lord rather than for people. Remember that the Lord will give you an inheritance as your reward and that the Master you are serving is Christ."
>
> (*NLT*, 1996, Colossians 3:23-24).

My challenge for you today beloved, is to see yourself as strong, capable, and worthy. Work hard at what you need to as if you were doing it for Christ. Make your Father proud of you. Show Him your hard-working heart. Show Him you can rise above any challenge, show Him that with His strength within your heart, you can do anything.

Each and every day, tend to your beautiful garden. Work hard on your heart, work hard on your character and work hard on your growth. The garden needs tending to, it needs sunshine, rain, trimming, cutting, and tearing down of weeds. The garden needs many different things to grow. In fact, it needs different seasons to thrive.

## CHAPTER NINE
### THE DAFFODIL MEADOW

The Daffodil meadow. Here I lay down. Here I find rest. Light, bright, and beautiful flowers surround me. I am peaceful, I am free. Up here in the daffodil meadow, I have a view of the world below. This hill is tall and wide, the air up here is fresher than down beneath the earth. Deeply I breathe in, slowly I breathe out. The gentle breeze brushes my nose as the air I breathe flows out of me. This breath I carry is from God. He breathed life into my lungs and I lay here alive, because of the Father. He got me through the coldest winter. He pulled me out of the dry, dead season I was in. It is springtime now, times have changed. I have changed and here I stay, in the daffodil meadow. Warmly I embrace the sunshine's rays. Softly the sun settles on my face, like a mother placing a blanket on her child. I feel protected and in harmony. I am safe here in the daffodil meadow. No one can hurt me, no one can find me. God and I sit here, in the meadow. Here my dreams are like a honeycomb, sweet and pure.

I dream of what my future will bring. I let the past fall back into the past, as I lay here in the daffodil meadow.

Again I breathe in, filling my lungs with the crisp spring air, and hold my breath for a moment. At this moment, time stops. Everything goes quiet. As I hold my breath, I begin to feel renewed and refreshed. Softly, I let the air trickle out of my lungs. I look up and see a bluebird soaring through the air, I had just breathed into. The air God placed for us to breathe in and out. The air that allows us to take a minute to pause, to slow down and calm our minds, is the same air the birds soar through the clouds. How I longed to be the bird at this moment, to watch as those below ran around in a rush. My life would slow down, my mind would stop and I would float across the bay of blue that surrounds the earth above.

Make the most of these deep breathing moments, where you can stop your racing mind. When you can go to the daffodil meadow. We need to all slow our lives down sometimes to take in all that is happening around us. When we find these hidden moments of peace within our days, we can begin to see God moving. He works in wonderful and mysterious ways, we need to take the time to hear from Him, spend time with Him and worship Him. His creation is a perfect example of how we can see Him. Look at the beautiful detail on a single flowers petal. The swirling of colors as they burst together in the center of the petal. Softly these colors merge into the bright green stem that holds them all together. As the wind blows them gently away, they float across the surface of the earth and find a place to rest peacefully until the sun dries them up, to be nothing but dust. The detail within the ocean, the sunsets, and the mountains above, all portray a loving Father that put so much detail into His creation. If He put that much detail into the earth around us, imagine how much detail He would put into creating you. His greatest treasure and most valued creation. The detail reminds me of His plan. How could He put this much detail in, if He did not have a plan for you? He carefully places you where you need to be. You need to rely on Him, spend time with Him and listen to where He is calling you to go. Trust that He will take care of His precious child and will never let you go. So I encourage you to remember how precious you are, how loved you are and how adored you are. Spend time with the Lord and slow down.

A daffodil's seed is ideally planted in winter, so it can grow its roots strong to flourish in Spring. When I was on a peaceful walk with some dear friends, we came across a street that was completely dead. The leaves on the trees were all gone. Even the branches looked like life had been sucked out of them. But then we came across a small patch of daffodils. They were even more beautiful during this dead winter season because they stood out so much. The bright colors that were seen from the end of the street, showed beauty and growth. We were in awe of these amazing flowers.

Have you ever planted a beautiful daffodil seed in your life during the winter season? All you can see is dead plants around you, all you can feel is the cold, brittle winter's wind slicing into you as it passes by. You planted something good into your heart, you worked so hard to keep it alive, to see it sprout up. Yet you are still in the early stages of the winter season. The daffodil's time has not come. While you cannot see it, the flower is setting itself up to blossom very soon. Deep within the surface of the earth are strong, healthy roots being formed ready for the flower to arrive. It is hard during these times to stay patient and hopeful as there are no signs of life during these winter times. But hidden deep within, there is life. There is an abundant life ready to flow and grow. It is more than you could have dreamed of or pictured. The daffodil meadow may be empty now, but it is about to flourish with endless daffodils. Filling your life with all the hope, love, and restoration you could ever need.

Make sure to plant these seeds during the early stages of your winter season. During your toughest times and in your sorrow, plant good seeds for you will reap what you sow. Those who stay bitter in their winter, will not plant good seeds. In fact, underneath their soil is nothing. They do not have a scenic daffodil sprouting and growing. When the seasons change for them, there will not be new life. The river of life will be empty for them and they will feel lost. Jealousy may sprout from within them as they look over at your garden and see the elegant, picturesque daffodil meadow. They reaped what they sowed, which was nothing good or beautiful. Their soil was empty. If you sow good things, when the season changes, you will see the beautiful new growth arrive. You will finally see your hard work coming to life as you begin to live the life God has for you. The seasons are always changing and will always come back around. When you reap the seeds you sowed from winter, you will see the abundance. Next time winter rolls around, instead of falling into a bitter way, plant good seeds for your future. When the winter arrives for another year, you will have the wisdom you need to make the best of this season. You cannot skip this season or hide away from it. It will come, it needs to come. It has to come for the growth of your garden. You have the choice of whether you are going to plant good seeds during this time or if you are going to plant bitter, sour seeds that have no way of prospering.

> "Don't be misled—you cannot mock the justice of God. You will always harvest what you plant. Those who live only to satisfy their own sinful nature will harvest decay and death from that sinful nature. But those who live to please the Spirit will harvest everlasting life from the Spirit. So let's not get tired of doing what is good. At just the right time we will reap a harvest of blessing if we don't give up."
>
> (NLT, 1996, Galatians 6:7-9).

This verse is powerful and speaks truth and life, it shows the effect planting good seeds has over your life. It can completely transform your next season. You will reap the harvest of blessings if you stay faithful and continue to allow Christ to work through your life. The notion of seasons is an interesting topic that may change your perspective of what you may be going through right now. Your hardships may actually be a hidden blessing and treasure for you. It may even be what you were praying for, yet you didn't realize it would come about in this form. The hardships are like the cold, painful winters where it seems your garden is dead. You feel as if it is dead and it looks dead too. You may have been stuck in a painful winter for weeks, months, or even years. You cannot see the season changing. You cannot see the hope that is just ahead. You have planted good seeds, and they are growing deep under the ground, but you are stuck in the winter season, longing for it to change.

These dark times can help you to realize the importance of light. They may bring many disappointments and tears, but know that these times are needed for the restoration of your heart and bring healing for you. You may be feeling lost and alone, but it is in this loneliness you find union with Christ. You may be feeling numb with grief, but you will soon understand the full extent of what joy is. You are becoming the person you were created to be and it is a beautiful story that is unfolding. As you grow and flourish, you will look back and be grateful for your toughest times, as it was those times that shaped you into the person that you are. If you prayed whole-heartedly for wisdom and strength, you may need to go through very tough times to receive these gifts. For it is through the testing of your faith that resilience and perseverance can flourish.

Stay strong during these hard times and keep your eyes on Jesus, for He will take care of you. The season will not last forever. No season does.

"For you know that when your faith is tested, your endurance has a chance to grow".

(*NLT,* 1996, James 1:3).

Eternal sunshine can actually cause destruction as drought will occur. If someone is in a continuous sunshine season, they will have no growth or life. The eternal sun will cause them pain. The rain needs to come every so often to bring growth and life back into your garden. The rain washes away the old and brings forward new hopes and new opportunities. If you had a dramatic change in your life or something tragic brought great change to your world, know that this rain that has come will actually bring life back into your garden. You may have gotten comfortable in the season of sunshine and when the rain came, you felt lost and disoriented. This is a good thing, it means growth and change are coming into your life. How you are feeling right now cannot last an eternity. We are constantly changing, growing, and moving through different seasons and changes. You may feel the pain that is constant and agonizing, but I can assure you, a new season is coming. They always do.

Oh, how I sometimes long to be a child again. When my heart was pure, my mind was innocent. The greatest pain and grief of adulthood wouldn't haunt me day by day. People's *words have power*. People's words can bring life or death to a person.

"The tongue can bring death or life;
those who love to talk will *reap* the consequences".

(*NLT*, 1996, Proverbs 18:21).

Even within your words, you can plant good seeds. The tongue is so powerful that the words you speak over yourself and others can have deep, lasting effects. Either for good or for bad. I have experienced words of death spoken over me. Words that I am worthless, unwanted, and a sinner. These words have the power to break me or harm my identity in Christ. These words come from the mouth of the enemy. They are vicious, they are malicious and I pray I do not turn out like the people who have spoken these words over me.

*Hurt people, hurt people.*

Yet there is always a choice. A choice to let the words into your heart or rise above it. If you are hurting, you have the choice of whether you are going to pass this hurt onto others. Even if deep within your soul you are broken, you can still choose to show love and kindness towards others. Slowly, and surely these kind acts will begin to mend your tender heart. Speak positive words of affirmations over your life. Know your identity is found in Jesus. Repeat these to yourself:

*I am not who they say I am. I am who Christ says I am. I am worthy, I am loved. I am more than enough. These words spoken over me have no hold over my heart. I am stronger than this, I will not allow them to break me down. They have not broken me, I cannot be broken, for the Holy Spirit lives within me. The same power that raised Jesus Christ from the dead lives within me. I can overcome anything. Nothing can break me, for Christ is my warrior. He is my shield and my strength.*

*I am braver and stronger now because of the words spoken over me. They caused me to rise up, be a better person than I was before. No weapon formed against me will prosper. For I know my heart, God created it. The words they say do not live within my heart any longer. They have been taken away by the Creator of the universe and are no longer having a hold over me.*

Do not allow words spoken over you to become you. If you do, then you will end up just like the people who talk badly about you. You will soon catch yourself talking critically about them. You are stronger than this, you do not need to become the people who bully you. You can become something better and stronger from this. You can rise above, you can grow. You are so beautiful inside and out, do not allow the words of others to determine who you are.

You know who you are. You know your worth. It is found in Christ. He says you are:

"For we are God's masterpiece. He has created us anew in Christ Jesus, so we can do the good things he planned for us long ago".

(*NLT*, 1996, Ephesians 2:10)

The following story was told to me during a morning devotion at work. It is a great analogy about the power of the tongue. Thank you for the work colleagues who brought this inspiration to me, it got me thinking and reflecting and I am grateful I am able to include it within this book. I hope you can reflect on this fiction story and see how it can affect your day-to-day conversations with others. It was exaggerated to bring the issue of the tongue to life and is not a true story.

\*\*\*

There once was a woman who was caught in the cycle of gossip. She was a kind and thoughtful member of a church and always had a beautiful servant heart. Deep down, however, she found joy in gossip. It comforted her spirit, made her feel more worthy. She felt so lost inside, that the only

way she could connect with the other women in the church was to make up stories and gossip. She had a terrible habit of it and she was tormented by her shame and guilt. She knew her words were not true, yet she had no idea how destructive her words really were. One day she went to her Pastors house for dinner. She said to him that she wanted to be healed from her gossiping. She found herself constantly speaking badly of others behind their back. The Pastor asked her to meet him at the church the following day as he was going to teach her a beautiful lesson about the effects of the tongue.

The next day they arrived at church. The woman had

just come from a coffee catch-up with the ladies from church. Together they laughed and told stories of the mistakes people within the church were making. The woman began to realize her words were quite hurtful, but she continued to talk badly about others as it was amusing for her and her friends. They talked badly about people so often, that the extent to how painful their words really were had been minimized within their own hearts. Judging those around them and laughing at their mistakes or choices brought them joy. The Bible is very clear about judging others:

"For in the same way you judge others, you will be judged, and with the measure you use, it will be measured to you".

(*NLT*, 1996, Matthew 7:1).

These words are like the weed analogy- they grow everywhere and anywhere. There is no end to them. They sprout up in all different places and cause pain and destruction all around. There has to be a stop to this gossip, especially within churches.

As the woman walked into the church building she was welcomed with a large basket of feathers. It was the middle of winter and it was a very windy day outside. The Pastor asked the woman to keep her coat on as they were going to the field across the road. There he asked the woman to gently place the feathers onto the field. Counting how many she placed down. When she was finished, she told the Pastor the number of feathers she had released. He said, "Well done, you were so careful about where you put the feathers and had such control over where they landed. Until the wind picked up. Now they are all scattered across the oval. Would you collect every feather back up now? Make sure you have the exact amount you gave away." He said.

"I can't do that. The majority of them have already blown away in the wind. They are out of my reach now." Said the woman.

"So, you were careful where you placed them. However, the second you placed them, they no longer were in your control. Did you know how light a feather was? Did you know that it drifts softly and easily through the wind?" Said the Pastor.

"Yes, I knew they wouldn't stay where I put them." She said with her head towards the ground. She was beginning to see the connection.

"Then why do you gossip behind people's backs when you know the words you say are like feathers floating in the wind?" Said the Pastor.

"I never thought about it like that. My words can be changed and spread around just like these feathers. Once they are spoken, they cannot be retrieved either. Thank you, I understand the power of the tongue." Said the woman.

The woman walked away with a new perspective.

\*\*\*

Be encouraged by this story to be mindful of what you

say to others. While actions are also highly important, it is the tongue that holds great power, as it determines your steps.

Speak kindly to others, but also speak kindly to yourself. While the tongue holds great power, so do the words you say to yourself in your mind. If your mind is continuously judging, and thinking poorly of others, sooner or later, your tongue will catch up with such thoughts and you will be saying things you may regret. Likewise, this leads to actions that you may also regret. Stay strong, stay mindful, and always look to grow in this area as it helps bring peace to your heart. If you know you hold your tongue and your thoughts are of a peaceful nature, then what others say about you will not matter to you. You will know deep down in your heart that you are not in the wrong and that you and God know the truth.

**CHAPTER TEN**

THE GARDEN OF YOUR HEART

When I was about 19-years-old I was living within a beautiful home in stunning Australia. There were vines that spiraled around the entrance. The garden was on a hill and had multiple levels to it. There were many flowers and plants that little butterflies would land on and flutter their elegant wings.

During the summertime, I bought a blowup swimming pool to make it through the scorching hot Australian summers. On those extremely hot days, I would take my pool to the shade of the garden and lay within the pool. The ice-cold water surrounded my body as I began to feel cooler. This was a moment of peace I will always be grateful for. Serenely I would lay in this pool with classical music playing in my ears. Classical music was something I held close to my heart as I was a ballet dancer. It brought peace and restoration to my soul as it connected me to the

Father. During my hard times in my early adult years, classical music was a major aspect that got me through.

One cold, winters evening I was driving home from a Bible study session. This particular night ran longer than usual as we were so caught up in the Word and prayer session, we all lost track of time. The drive home was 20 minutes, so I had a good playlist of classical music playing to get me home. By the time I reached home, it was 11:20 pm, I was ready to turn my heater on and jump straight into bed. Pulling into the driveway, my heart was not on high alert for danger as I had just had an incredible fellowship night with people from church. My heart was light and my mind was calm. However, I noticed something strange as I pulled into my quiet dark street. One thing you should know is that the street was very noiseless and shadowy. There were not many street lights on as it was a back street off one of the main streets. It was hard to tell what the shadow figure was. As I got closer, I realized it was a man dressed in all black. My naive mind did not register that I was in danger, instead, I did not even realize the time and just thought the man was out for an evening winter walk.

The closer I got, the more I could see the man. He was carrying a long, big stick that he held with a firm grip. He had a torch on, but it was very dim. Gently I put my blinker on, as I saw the man walk out of my driveway, down the slight hill, and onto the street. I was alone that night, the house had no one else in it. Looking back I realized that I should not have turned into my driveway and instead, I could have called one of the Bible study members and told them there was a suspicious man outside my house.

However, I continued to pull into the driveway confidently. As I looked into my rearview mirror, I watched as the man walked in the opposite direction to my house. This calmed me.

*Lord, please protect me, let me get into the house safely tonight.*

As I was living alone, I sometimes forgot to leave the light on for myself. This particular night, it was very dark and I couldn't quite see anything. So before I even hopped out of the car, I turned my phone torch on, looked to see that the man was in the opposite direction, and started to make a game plan. With this house, I lived in the flat down under the house. My door was just around the corner, about a 10-15 meter walk. I undid my seat belt. Said another prayer and I hopped out of the car. My eyes did not leave the man's torch. I closed the door gently, but it still made a loud *bang*. The moment the door closed, I watch as the torch started running back towards me. The man heard my door and he was coming back. He knew I was alone, he knew no one else was in the house.

Quickly I locked my car door and raced for my house door. My mind went blank, my heart pounded out of my chest. The man was running towards me. Fear, panic, and anxiety flooded my entire body and I was shaking. I have far too many keys on my key chain so it was a struggle to find my keys. As I fiddled with the keys my mind continually repeated,

*Please, Jesus, protect me, please Jesus protect me.*

I finally got the key I needed as I heard the footsteps coming towards me. I opened the door and with a slam, I closed it. Then I locked it as quickly as I could. The room was spinning. I was trapped in the house, with a man outside who knew I was alone. Quickly I ran upstairs to check all the windows were closed and the doors were locked. My body felt like it was floating on a cloud. I no longer felt like I was on earth anymore, I was drifting into a panicked state.

Frantically I closed every window as tightly as I could. Checking every door in the house.

*Why are there so many windows in this house?*

Eventually, everything was locked up. Instead of turning on the TV and the lights. I made everything silent and I ran to my room. I curled up into a little ball on my bed and sat in the dark. The house had never been this quiet, every noise haunted me.

My heart started pounding. He could come in at any moment.

*He probably knows I am down here. He knows I am alone.*

Eventually, I called my parents who lived in a different

city as that was all my mind could rationally think to do. As I was on the phone with them, I walked upstairs. Walking into a dark room where a man could be waiting to harm you was a terrifying thing. As I silently tip-toed up, I walked to the front of the room where I could see the man still there. By the window, he was trying to break in.

My father called the police for me and the police eventually arrived. I was looked after and the police took care of the man. While I was not physically harmed, the emotional distress that flowed from this experience was immense and sparked the beginning of a hard season for me. I'm going to share my journey to healing from this experience.

The following days that passed by were numb, my body had not fully comprehended what had happened. At night time my mind would replay the scenario, over and over again. Every time I relived it, I felt the same pounding heartbeat. My mind would go into the fog again and my stomach would have that feeling where it dropped and it took a few moments to catch my breath again.

Soon there were sleepless nights, I began to stay awake as a protection mechanism to not allow myself to be in a vulnerable position. My thought,

*If I am awake, I can protect myself, if I allow myself to sleep, harm and danger will come my way.*

Here was where I went wrong. The determination of my safety was no longer put in God's hands but in my own. To an extent, we should be cautious, mindful, and careful.

I, however, was in a safe place, the doors were all locked and no one could get in.

It is in these safe places that we need to completely hand everything over to God. I did my part, now it was time to let God step in and keep me safe.

I would say this prayer:

*Jesus, I give everything and everyone to you. I give everything and everyone to you.*

When the stress would come, I found the best thing for me was to take deep breathes and walk around the room. Listening to classical music, or putting the tv on, I would catch my breath again and allow myself to slow my heart rate.

*Breathe in, wait four seconds, breathe out, wait four seconds.*

Over and over I repeated this until I could begin to breathe again. It is always good to speak up if you are experiencing moments like these. Talk to someone wise, who you can trust, and who will be there for you when you need someone to listen.

As the years passed by, my pain towards this situation began to fade. Time really does heal all wounds. This was something that took a lot of patience and resilience to accept. Work hard at getting through the tough times, stay strong, patient and give all that you can over to the Lord.

Beloved, you are strong and you can make it through this season you are in. Allow yourself to speak up if you need to. Give your pain, worries, and hurt to God. He cares so deeply for you.

One peaceful summers day, I drove an hour to visit Jeremey and his family. They lived on a beautiful property in the Australian countryside. Their house had the most magnificent balcony that overlooked the mountains. Each night the sky painted a beautiful picture with yellows, pinks, blues, and oranges. God blessed this family with an elegant painting each night. Jeremy's sister Lily and I would sometimes go out onto the balcony to look at the beautiful sunset. It was these moments that I hold onto and treasure. The moments when time stands still and you are standing out in the warm summer night air taking in the breathtaking views that God hand-painted for me and Lily. Together we would pause and take it in, enjoying the incredible views.

During the winter seasons, you could see the snow on the mountains in the distance and it was pure bliss.

On this same summer's day, Jeremey, his sister Lily and I went into their garden to tend to it. Now their garden was magnificent. They had a vegetable garden that was filled with rosemary, tomatoes, strawberries, and many other great fruits and vegetables. They had all kinds of fruit trees too. But the best part of the garden was their rose bushes. Lily would always cut a special rose for me when I visited. This was such a beautiful, kind and thoughtful act of her to do.

My middle name is Rose and I have always had a soft spot for roses. Her rose garden was one of the best rose gardens I had ever seen. When we walked through the garden, I would take a deep breath in, look over at the beautiful countryside and smile to God for the blessing of being in such a beautiful country, peaceful garden and enjoying time with this precious friend.

While gardening, we had hats, shorts, and t-shirts on. It was a scorching hot Australian summer's day. I could feel my body overheating and my mouth began to feel dry. I liked this feeling, this Australian summer feel. The grass was quite dry, but we were determined to rip up all the weeds and create a beautiful new garden bed. This was Jeremy's part of the garden. I loved the way they shared their garden. What made this garden even more picturesque was that it backed onto a stunning bush walk, up onto a wonderful hill. The view from the top was magnificent and always made me feel closer to God.

As we had music playing, I was singing in my head and got lost in the songs. You would say I was in my happy place, I was distracted, I was content and I was delighted to be gardening. No thoughts of harm or danger were in my mind.

Suddenly, within a moment, Lily dug up a large spider. Without even realizing it, she flinched and the spider sprung over to my bare arm. I felt it crawling up my arm and with a *scream,* I flicked it over towards Jeremey. Hoping he would know what to do, he stayed very calm and guided the little (which I thought was quite big, as I am afraid of spiders) back to a safe place.

You see, spiders are needed in the garden. They are part of a system. Every animal has a purpose and a reason for being created. God has a plan for every insect, every bird, and even every spider. It is part of our ecosystem.

When things that are unfamiliar come into our hearts and we do not know what to do, but to flick it out of our garden, we may be harming ourselves more than we realized. The spider would have been more afraid of us than we were of him. Sometimes life will bring challenges, deeper thoughts, heavier topics, greater life experiences to grow us and challenge us.

There is a purpose and a plan for you. There is no experience that God cannot turn into good. God already knew the spider was there when we set out to the garden. I even expected there to be some bugs. However, I still felt a great shock when it arrived. When challenges come, they may come as a shock or surprise. Know that God has a beautiful plan for your life. Even if you cannot see at the moment why a giant spider would jump out and crawl up your arm, there may be a greater reason. The spider had a purpose in that garden. As do our challenges and heartbreaks, they have a purpose to serve, in the garden of your heart.

God will take care of you and watch over you. Especially during hard times in your life. Note that I was in my own happy world when trouble came. It surprised me and made me realize that anything can happen. The experience allowed me to see that life is always growing and changing. New things are always ahead. The seasons will always change. The heartbreak will heal. The pain will fade and the brokenness will mend. God will care for you.

Now Lily was an incredible cook. She would make the

most amazing meals but the best things she would make were desserts. Her Turkish delight cheesecake was out of this world. The rose water flavor made the dish a marvelous taste that melted in your mouth.

Cooking for others is a benevolent, sacrificial act of kindness. When someone is hurting, going through something, or needs extra support a home-cooked meal or dessert will always have a positive effect on those around you. Blessings others should be a priority in your life as we are called to be servant-hearted and to be like Jesus. Putting others first and thinking more about how to make those around you happy will inevitably enhance your heart's spirits. You will experience a different kind of joy, a selfless God-given joy will begin to flourish in your heart. This reminded me of the noble Bible verse which tells us live as a sacrifice to the Lord.

I encourage you, to live as a sacrifice for the Lord and seek out ways you can bless others and brighten their days.

You see, when you bring joy to others, you are actually planting a lovely seed within your own garden. Your heart has become that little bit sweeter. The bitter weeds will begin to fade away. You will start to see yourself in a brighter and more life-filled light. As you see, you have the capability of blessing others, the way Jesus did.

You have a kind, pure heart within. Even if you find yourself judging others, speaking poorly about them, or causing pain. Deep within, you have a lovely garden that has hidden treasures. Unleash your inner beauty to the world around you and show them how lovely your garden truly is.

\*\*\*

"And so, dear brothers and sisters, I plead with you to give your bodies to God because of all he has done for you. Let them be a living and holy sacrifice—the kind he will find acceptable. This is truly the way to worship him. Don't copy the behavior and customs of this world but let God transform you into a new person by changing the way you think. Then you will learn to know God's will for you, which is good and pleasing and perfect."

(NLT, *1996*, Romans 12-1).

The garden of your heart is something to cherish. Each and every day you need to make a conscious decision about how you will treat your garden that day. Will you tend to it gently and remove the weeds of lies? Or will you allow yourself to get tangled up in the weeds? Work hard at your garden, but work hard at it with the Lord and for the Lord. He is with you always and He longs to guide you on your journey.

Every garden is given the most precious gift of all, the gift of Grace. This gift means you can walk in freedom, despite your past. You can live freely and confidently knowing that the Lord loves you and will always be with you.

You, my beloved, have a bright future ahead. Allow the Lord to work on the garden of your heart. Let Him in and see the transformation He can bring to you. Your garden is so beautiful. It's time you gave up your old ways. It's time to step into your garden of Grace.

**CHAPTER ELEVEN**

THE FLOWER OF FORGIVENESS

In the spring of 2009, I was about to embark on a wonderful adventure. Within the playground of my British school, I ran from the hidden forest all the way down to the Year 1 playground. You see, this was a race to see who was the fastest in the Year 4 class. I came in the top 3 and was very excited about it. The next contest was going to be a singing contest to see who was the most talented singer. My friends and I asked the teacher if we could hold a talent show on the Friday of that week. When she agreed, we all got straight into our training as well as decorating the classroom to make it a talent show environment. Down the back of the playground, near the hidden forest was an abandoned stage. It was made of wood and had vines exploding out of it. When I stood upon the stage I began to sing one of my favorite songs. The only song I knew perfectly off by heart, the song *Hallelujah*. The rest of the week I practiced the song out in the garden on the trampoline. My neighbor Eden was an amazing singer and she gave me some tips. Eden and I had a count down till the talent show because we were both so excited to see what the talent show day would bring.

Before I knew it, Friday had come. It was the day of the big talent show and I was over the moon about it. I remember standing outside the classroom lining up for the class after the bell had gone. I was practicing my song with my friend Jessica. She told me to hold the high note longer so that I can win the talent show. As we walked into the classroom, I began to feel my palms sweating and I suddenly realized my sister might be right. Maybe I really was not a good singer and my friends were all playing a joke on me. I began to have a mini-meltdown. As we moved our chairs to the front of the room to create an audience, I began to worry that this was not the path I wanted to go down.

"Next up, we have Amelia." My teacher said, looking at me with a warm smile.

I saw everyone's eyes dart back to me and I realized, it was my time to sing. I went to the front of the room. I felt my hands shaking, my palms sweating and my heart pounding out of my chest. Suddenly, the room began to spin and I could not walk in a straight line. Slowly I took some deep breaths and made it to the front of the room. Looking out at my classmates, who sat in a semi-circle around me. My teacher was sitting at her desk in the corner of the room, she gave me a bright smile that made me feel confident and sure that I could do this. As I began to sing, I remembered how much I loved music and I closed my eyes and got right into the song. The time flew by and before I knew it, my song was over. I felt as though I was walking on air. I felt as light as a cloud.

*I did it, I really did it. That was the first time I had ever sung in front of the class.*

As I walked back to my chair, I felt confident with my performance. Only time will tell if I have won the contest. Next, we had a girl named Natasha. She was strong-willed, highly confident, and extremely talented. While I usually wouldn't think I'd have a chance against her, today seemed different.

*Maybe I could actually win, maybe I could prove my sister wrong.*

After Natasha's performance, we all took a vote. I smiled as I looked across at my friends. I voted for them to get top 3 prizes as we were best friends, I knew they would vote for me as well. Soon we were let out for lunch and my teacher was counting the votes while we ate in the dining hall.

As I got my home-cooked meal and sat down in the dining hall, all my mind could think of were the results of the talent show. For some reason, I had my heart set out to make the top 3. This would be a day to remember if I could show my family I really could sing.

"Who did you all vote for?" Said my bubbly friend Sophie.

"Well, we all voted for, Sarah, Oliver, and of course, Natasha for number one!" Said my best friend Rosemary.

"Wait, you didn't vote for me? It is okay if you didn't, I just thought we were voting for each other." I said with a tear in my eye.

"Oh sorry Amelia, we just had to vote for Natasha as number one, I'm sure you can understand, she was amazing. I mean, you were great and all, but no one can compare to Natasha." Said Rosemary.

"Yes, of course, I understand. I might go to the bathroom before the bell rings." I said as I began to walk confidently out the door. When I reached the bathroom, I began to tear up. While this was only a small betrayal, I felt pretty worthless and led on by my friends. I began to listen to the voice in my mind that told me I wasn't good enough. As I looked in the mirror, I no longer saw myself as someone strong and capable, I saw a weak girl who was wrong about her talents. I took a deep breath and headed back to the classroom as I heard the bell ring.

Walking into the classroom, I sat next to my best friends. While I smiled and pretended I was okay, I was actually feeling quite hurt from this experience. The teacher went up to the front and announced the top 3. While I can't remember the names of $3^{rd}$ and $2^{nd}$ position, I can clearly remember Natasha was the winner. I was happy for her, I really was. I just felt a little disappointed in my friends for leading me to think I was good and then not voting for me. While this was a tough week, what followed the next week was even more betrayal.

It was a Tuesday afternoon on a British winter's day

and we had just finished a literacy lesson. I was reading the book Hetty Feather by Jaqueline Wilson. This book was one I shall always treasure. It was heartbreaking, inspiring, and completely engaging. I would never want to put the book down. As the bell rang for the end of the day, I couldn't put my book down. I said bye to my friends and grabbed my bookbag, but left my desk a big mess. As I walked down the classroom steps, I was reading the final page of a thrilling chapter, I heard my teacher yell,

"Amelia, you come back here right this minute and clean your desk before you go home."

I was never the student to get in trouble so I was pretty shaken up when I heard this. I gasped and quickly ran back up the concrete stairs to the classroom. With my book in one hand and bag in the other, I tripped up the stairs, dropped my book, and landed on my left fingers facing towards the concrete. I heard a snap and suddenly couldn't feel any of my fingers on my left hand. My body went into shock and I was confused by what was happening. I looked up and my teacher had seen the whole incident take place. She gently grabbed my hand and helped me up. My fingers on my left hand began to have feeling and they throbbed, stabbed, and began to swell. I started to panic and slowly I walked into the classroom. My teacher stayed behind me and picked up my bag and book. I headed to my chair to tuck it in. With tears pouring down my face I began to clean up the mess I had made earlier that day.

"Never mind that I will fix it up for you, let's just get you to the nurse." My teacher graciously said.

"But I, but I need to," I said.

"Come on, let's go." She said with a smile but with a firm tone in her voice.

Briskly we walked all the way from the back of the school to the front and found the nurse. As she documented what had happened, I watched as my finger grew double the size. She put ice on them but that just made it hurt even more. They began to bruise up as the ice-cooled my fingers down. My mother was called and she came to the office immediately. We went to the emergency room and got my fingers X-rayed. I had broken my fingers on my left hand. The doctors taped them next to one another and gave me a sling. I went home that day to a relaxing evening of Hetty Feather reading and my favorite dinner cooked for me.

The next day at school everyone gathered around me to ask what had happened, I explained the story to them and showed them how swollen my fingers still were. Everyone signed my sling and I felt quite special if I'm honest. While it was a painful experience, I sure got well looked after by everyone. In the morning we took part in a clay-making and painting activity. We had already made the clay and it was time for painting. We were going to do one layer in the morning and another layer in the afternoon.

The painting was my favorite part of the week. I just loved creating new things and all the different colors we got to work with. I painted mine a beautiful pastel color with a pattern of blue, purple, and pink. These were and still are my favorite colors. On the bottom of my clay, I painted my initials "A.R" to make sure no one else thought it was there's. Then I put it at the back right corner of the drying rack so it would be safe. As the bell rang for recess we all went outside to the playground. I couldn't run around like I usually did with my broken fingers, so I sat on the abandoned stage with my friend Rosemary and told funny stories to each other. The stage was round the back of the school and was right near my Year 4 classroom.

"I'm going to the bathroom, I'll be back in a moment," Rosemary said.

As Rosemary left, I sat by the tree waiting for her. I picked a pretty flower and picked off each petal slowly singing a song in my head. As I looked up, I saw Natasha sneaking over towards our classroom. She was crouching below the window and looking around to see if anyone was watching her. I slipped behind the tree so she wouldn't see me. I watched as she snuck into the classroom. I couldn't quite see what she was doing, but she was in there for a while. When she came out, she had bright red and blue paint all over her hands. She tucked her hands behind her back and ran off to the bathroom. She almost ran into Rosemary as she was walking back towards me.

"Rosemary, I just saw Natasha sneak into the classroom," I said.

"Oh she probably forgot something, I wouldn't be concerned, Natasha is a really nice and kind girl, I am sure she wasn't up to anything," Rosemary said.

"Yeah, you're probably right, maybe I was thinking too much into this." I believed.

As the bell rang we went to the hall for sport. I couldn't

participate so I quickly walked back to the classroom to grab my Hetty Feather book while everyone was in the hall. As I grabbed it, I looked over at the clay drying area. I was a little confused why Natasha had paint on her hands. As I looked, I saw the pot that I had placed on the right-hand corner was covered in the bright red and blue paint that Natasha had on her hands. My stomach dropped, she had painted over the top of my clay. I looked on the bottom and you could see the outline of my initials "A.R" were still visible. *Why would she paint over the top of my clay? I am so mad at her for doing this.* I thought.

Quickly I held my book and ran back to the hall. I raced over to my teacher and told her what I had seen.

"Now dear, I think that is an unlikely story, for someone to sneak in without me seeing and paint over the top of your clay. Why would Natasha even do that? I think you are mistaken." My teacher said calmly.

"But, I can still see my initials, it was mine," I exclaimed.

"I'm sorry Amelia, but you are mistaken and this is not the time to be talking about this. Now go read your book in the corner and we will talk about it this afternoon when we are finishing art." She said with raised eyebrows and a firm look.

I nodded and walked with tears in my eyes over to the corner of the room to read my book. As I sat with my legs crossed in the corner of the hall, I looked over at Natasha. She was hanging out with my best friend Rosemary. She was taller, more talented, and more beautiful than I was. *Maybe my friends like her more than me. Maybe Natasha will replace me in my friendship group.* My spirits were fading and I was feeling pretty flat at this point. My fingers were aching and I wanted more than anything to just go home.

At lunch, I told the others what I saw and how Natasha had painted over my clay.

"Amelia, Rosemary was with you, she would have seen it if it was true." Said Sarah.

"But Rosemary was at the bathroom, only I saw it, and it was true. I wouldn't make this up." I said determinedly.

"I'm sorry but we just don't think this is something Natasha would do. I think you are mistaken. It might be because your fingers are sore and you are not thinking straight, but don't take it out on Natasha. She's pretty and nice and we all like her." Said Sarah.

"Maybe you are right." I gave up but I knew they were wrong.

When we went back to class I showed my friends the initials on the bottom of the clay and my teacher, no one would believe me because Natasha was the nice, perfect girl who never did anything wrong. I had never caused a scene like this before either, but after not tidying my desk the day before, my teacher was losing faith in me.

"You'll just have to paint a new one. I have a spare clay over here." Said, my teacher.

As I sat and painted a new one, with only one hand as my other hand was in a sling. I began to feel pretty resentful towards everyone as I had proof, yet no one believed me. Forgiveness was not at the top of my priorities.

People are going to let you down. We live in a fallen world that is broken, unforgiving, and hurtful at times.

People will even hurt you without even meaning to. We cannot control how others respond to our decisions or mistakes, but we can control what we do about it. If you have ever hurt someone, it is important to own your mistake and be confident that you have done the right thing. When someone hurts you, it is important to communicate with them how you are feeling. Sometimes allowing yourself a *cool-down time* is necessary to ensure you do not say something you would regret. When you cool down a little, you will allow your mind to be in a better headspace to think rationally and agree upon a solution to the problem that has occurred. God plays a major role in the conflict.

When someone hurts you deep within your core, if someone undermines your character or your identity in Christ, it is important to run back to Christ at this moment. If you allow their words to soak into your heart, you will become a person you did not intend to become. You slowly lose your sense of self and feed into the lies they are saying about you. When you are hurt deeply it is hard to see the bigger picture. It is also hard to forgive. Forgiveness is not about the other person's actions being justified, it is you letting them go. We all have people within *the pit of your heart,* these are the people you hold hostage until you get your apology or justification for their actions.

We all dig a hole in the garden of our hearts and place that person hidden deep within. Sometimes you bury their hurt so deeply that when you see them, you have a sense of resentment towards them but cannot quite put your finger on why they are there. A secret to learn with this pit analogy is that you did not actually put the person who caused you harm in the pit, you put yourself there.

You put your insecurities, your pain, your emotions, your reactions, and your hurt into the pit because you do not want to face it. You cover these up with the name of the person who hurt you. You may even tell yourself and others that this was done because of unforgiveness in your heart. I challenge you to take a look into your heart, who have you placed in a pit? When you look down into the pit, you will notice it is not actually them in there, but a mirrored reflection of you. All the things you wish you didn't say or do are in there. All the mistakes you made are in there. Yet you comfortably paint a sign with someone else's name on it and place it above the pit for all to see. You speak badly about this person behind their back or think negative thoughts towards them because you think it is them that are in the wrong. All they did was bring your deepest insecurities to the surface. They made you question your identity. Are you going to allow yourself to live this way? With an unforgettable heart that holds grudges and places people in a negative pit of your heart? Or are you going to deal with these pains, insecurities, and hurts that are hidden so deep within?

Sometimes they are so deep you don't even know they are there. You need to dig them up gradually and give them to God. Allow yourself to be set free from this. It starts by taking down that sign with someone else's name on it. This is the first act of forgiveness. When you realize, it is not about them, but it is about you. Once you take this sign down you realize the lie you are telling yourself, which is that they are the ones that made you feel this way. While yes, they may have brought your insecurities into the light and surfaced them before you were ready. But, this needed to happen so that you can give them to God, process them and move on with your life. Setting that person who wronged you free and allowing yourself to love others wholeheartedly even if they have wronged you is a healing process.

Forgiveness may be hard if you have a big, deep pit of hurt, regret, and insecurities to work through. Once you begin this process of healing and forgiving you will begin to see it is possible to set people free from unforgiveness, as none of this had anything to do with them. It had everything to do with you and your own heart.

Ask God to set you free and ask Him to guide you as you forgive those who hurt you. Forgiveness is an important topic as it is something Christ is very familiar with. The debt we owe Christ is our life. We have wronged Him more than we could have ever wanted to, yet He forgives us wholeheartedly and loves us unconditionally.

Christ forgives us, and so we should forgive those who hurt us. When we set people free we will feel free as we truly understand what Christ has done for us. A passage to look into is Matthew 18:21-22. I will share a small part of it, but I encourage you to go deeper into this story as you learn just how much God has set us free from.

"Then Peter came to Him and asked, "Lord, how often should I forgive someone who sins against me? Seven times?"

"No, not seven times," Jesus replied, "but seventy times seven."

(NLT, *1996*, Matthew 18:21-22).

## Reflection

1. Do you find forgiveness can be challenging at times?
2. Who is someone you need to forgive and let go of?

**CHAPTER TWELVE**

THE REGROWTH AND REGRET

The year I was 21-years-old, I packed up my bags and moved to the country for the final term of the school year. I had been working with this wonderful country school all throughout the year. I used to travel from my city to the school each day. This was only about 2 hours of driving a day. However, with the upcoming pandemic, there were restrictions and rules against me traveling back and forth. So I had to make the decision for what my final 3 months of the year would look like. When the idea of moving to the country came to mind, I was immediately excited and thrilled that this opportunity had come. Growing up in a small British village, I had always had a connection to the country and the lifestyle of a smaller community. With ten years of suburban city life in my blood, I knew I needed a change, I needed to go back to the country.

The staff at the school I was working at were abundantly amazing and kind. Many of them offered up their homes for me to stay at. Each home was unique and precious in its own way. One home was right by the river. As I walked out onto their deck, I looked up to a magnificent green hill that took my breath away. Slowly I would close my eyes and take in deep breaths. Capturing the beauty of this location. The river was found at the bottom of this hill and was full from all the rain that had come that season. With the constant rushing of water peacefully drifting past me, like the memories of my childhood, I found this brought closure and peace to my heart.

Life had brought many ups and downs within this year. Many pains, heartbreaks, and losses. Yet, all of that led me to that moment by the river. That exact moment where I was given the privilege of staying at such a beautiful location. It was in this moment a peace washed over me, a peace I had never experienced. The pain and worries of that year felt as if they had been thrown into the river in front of me. Intently I watched as the water crashed against the rocks, each hurt, pain, and heartbreak I had experienced that year was now in that stunning river. It was being taken away from me. I was moving on from it and I was able to let it go. Deeply I breathed in, slowly I breathed out. This was a moment I would always hold onto. The moment I let my past be in the past and watched it drift down the river out of my sight, for all eternity. Even if I go back to the river, the water I had seen that day was already gone. New fresh icy cold, melted snow appeared before me. New memories had arrived and I could now smile for the pain of the past was now in my past, washed away by the river of life.

God had new opportunities ahead of me and I could finally have peace knowing I could heal from the pains of this life. The next house was a thirty-minute drive out of town. The road was long but brought a sense of bliss. The house was beautiful and simple. It was a cottage in the bush, located right below a hill. Each night I would need to walk out into the bush to collect sticks and leaves for my fire. This was my only source of heat, during some very cold nights. With a cozy lounge room and upstairs bedroom, I felt very at home and comforted within this house. God was so evident within this season of my life. Having come from a past of panic attacks when living alone, I was amazed I never lost sight of Christ. I never got afraid, never worried, and felt extremely peaceful throughout my time in this house. I was located in the snowy mountains of rural NSW. On the drive into town, I could look over my left shoulder and see picturesque snow out on the distant mountains. As I got closer to the shops, I could smell the freshly cut grass seeping into the cracks of the car. Deeply I breathed in, slowly I breathed out. The fresh country air had a hold over me and made me feel instantly calm and collected. My favorite spot on the drive was the canola field. Millions of stunning yellow canola growing. Right behind the yellow field were two large hills. Each evening as I drove home, I would time my drive to watch the sun going down right between those two hills. With the sparkle of the radiant sun hidden deep within the crests of the mountains, I took in the blissful scene of yellow canola fields and golden sunshine. A few times the scene was so beautiful I pulled my car over to take it all in. This was a time to be thankful to God. Prays of gratefulness and thanksgiving were spoken at the canola field.

Getting to where I was at this point in my life, required many hardships to shape my heart. I needed a lot of growing up to do that year and a lot of change occurred. I made many mistakes that I regret and held so tightly to. Sometimes when I was driving, the regrets of things that occurred months before would creep into my mind like a gust of wind. Blowing away all other thoughts. Sometimes I felt I had no control over the thoughts I was having. I would try to push them away but then I realized I needed to feel that way to process the past. Sometimes, you need to allow the pain to come to move forward from it. It was healthy for the past regrets to come to my mind, it meant my heart was feeling safe, secure, and ready to process all that I had been through. When I allowed those memories to take a hold of me, I would pray and listen to what my heart was saying. This helped me to grow, move on and realize I was no longer the person from the past. I was a new creation in Christ and my heart had been transformed since that day. Grief and pain are something that does not go away easily, yet you can learn to process it and create a new reality to move forward with a scar in your heart. You take past regrets and learn from them. Never turn back to the old person you once were. Take this regret and use it to be transformed and become a new creation. Many times I would even process words that should not have been said to someone I loved dearly or the deafening silence of the unspoken words I held back from saying. These silent words haunted my heart. Words are powerful and sometimes we say the wrong thing, sometimes we forget to say the right thing. All we can do is move forward, learn from the mistakes and do better next time. It is an awful

feeling knowing that you hurt someone without even realizing it. Own your regrets and mistakes. Apologize for them and move forward. Never sit in the pit of regret, for you can never truly move forward until you allow yourself to do so.

One cold night in the country cabin, I had gotten home late from a dinner with friends from work. They had a beautiful house that was located on the top of a hill. As you arrived inside their amazing garden, you needed to walk through an arbor that was covered in vines. As you sliced through the overgrown vines, you discovered an incredible garden that took your breath away. The views out into the snowy mountains were indescribable. The owners of the house invited me to join them in their spa. It was an unforgettable night. Sitting within the hot, steaming tub, the LED lights shimmering against the flowing water. As I let my head tilt back, I saw the stars in a new light. I had never seen the sky look this magnificent. The stars shone brighter than I had ever seen. The family explained the sky looks even brighter out in the country as there are no city lights to contrast against the night lights in the sky. It made me realize, this was how the sky was supposed to look. God intended the sky to shine as brightly as it did that night. The world was not initially created with city street lights and restaurant lights blocking the beauty of the natural night sky. I took a deep breath in and took a picture with my memory. To take a picture with your memory is a magical thing to do. All you need to do is stare at the view you are trying to capture for about ten seconds. Then you close your eyes for three seconds, picturing the scene you were just looking at. By doing this activity you are changing the memory from a generic memory to a more significant memory. It actually moves into a different part of your brain and is easier to recall as time passes. I would never forget that night, the night the sky reflected the warmth and covering of a naturally beautiful sky.

As we headed home, I had the simplistic bliss of the night's sky imprinted in my mind. Thinking of such a peaceful evening, I had a light-hearted feeling in my spirit. Driving home with a dear friend of mine, we talked about life and the deeper aspects of our worries and fears for the future. It was one of those conversations that leaves you feeling peaceful and as if you have taken a weight off your shoulder. Walking back into my home, I suddenly realized, I had to be brave that night as there was a mouse in my house. With a deep fear of mice, I was needing to pray as I walked in the door and try to keep my mind on the beautiful night's sky and forget about my worries. I had a shower, got ready for bed, and tucked myself in. Forgetting about the mouse, I fell asleep quite peacefully. At around 12:30 pm, I heard a loud noise above me. I reached for the light switch, which was accessible from my bed. The second I turned on the light, I suddenly looked up and saw a giant rat crawling down the wall towards me.

I screamed a scream I had never heard come from my mouth. Suddenly, the rat launched itself onto my bed and went for the heat pack that was above my head. Aggressively it nibbled on the wheat from the heat pack and didn't even seem phased by me. I grabbed my keys, jumper, shoes and ran out the door to the car. Quickly turned the light out on my way through. I was shaking as I sat in the car and called my mother. Unsure of what to do next, I needed to calm myself down. While rats are not that dangerous and would never harm me, I just had such a big fright from the rat coming towards me. We decided I would drive to a friend's house and stay the night there. Safely, I went to sleep at a friend's house, with rats and mice on my mind.

Sometimes I wonder why many are born with fears of animals that are actually harmless towards us. Rats just want food and a warm place to sleep. They truly do not come into people's homes to attack or cause any harm to us. The enemy evokes similar qualities to this. While the enemy comes into our hearts to hurt us and deceive us. The thing that makes the enemy similar is that he has no power over us and cannot actually bite us. While he makes a loud roar and says a few lies, he cannot touch us or impact us if we do not allow him. With the Holy Spirit living within your heart, a born-again Christian does not need to live in fear from the enemy for he is as harmless as a toothless lion. You can laugh at his roars as they are not as scary as he wants you to believe. The devil has no sharp teeth to touch the children of God, only a voice to deceive. We have a choice whether we want to live in fear and allow a toothless lion to impact our lives, or step into the freedom of Christ.

Your heart is a precious thing, I hope you know that God truly did make you, loves you, and plans the best path ahead for you. May this book guide you, challenge you and encourage you on your journey ahead. Faith is a process and an up and down aspect of life that has different seasons and times. With each new season, I pray you to plant the seeds of righteousness, hope, love, joy, peace, patience, kindness, goodness, gentleness, strength, and courage. Live each day for Christ. Learn from your past mistakes and always know, the garden of your heart is a place full of grace, wonder, and beauty. The Lord can do miraculous things within the garden of your heart. Step into your garden of grace as you walk this journey with the Lord.

"Within the white gate, is a beautiful place. With her beauty, she captivates this space. For the Lord has blessed her with unconditional love. Gently He fills her with peace from above. Warmly she takes His embrace, knowing her worth is found in her, *Garden of Grace.*"

**(Raymond, 2021)**

## ACKNOWLEDGMENTS

I'd like to thank Esther for the illustrations. Abigail for editing the manuscript. Laura for her amazing photography. Peter, for doing the final edit. And to my family and friends for their encouragement and support.

**REFERENCES**

*Holy Bible, New Living Translation.* (1996). Tyndale House Publisher.

Potter, B. (1901). The Tale of Peter Rabbit. Warne.

Wilson, J. (2009). Hetty Feather. Yearling Publisher.

**Amelia Raymond**
*Snowy Mountains Christian School*

Growing up as a Pastors daughter, Amelia Raymond was always surrounded by a community of Christians to uplift her and encourage her faith. With many Christian women to look up to, Amelia draws inspiration from those women within her parents' church.

Amelia is now a Primary teacher that longs to one day write Christian children's books to share within
her own classroom. With her cousin as an illustrator, Amelia has many upcoming plans for further books to write and create.

Garden of Grace was inspired by Holy Scriptures. All references to the Scriptures are to bring life and encouragement to this book. To lead readers towards the Bible and to look to Christ as their ultimate inspiration and guidance.

www.ingramcontent.com/pod-product-compliance
Lightning Source LLC
Chambersburg PA
CBHW042226160426
42811CB00117B/1021